THE *American Political Process*

THE AMERICAN IMAGE SERIES
Ernest R. May, General Editor

THE AMERICAN SOCIETY
Edited by Kenneth S. Lynn

THE AMERICAN FOREIGN POLICY
Edited by Ernest R. May

THE AMERICAN POLITICAL PROCESS
Edited by Leonard W. Levy and John P. Roche

THE AMERICAN ECONOMY
Edited by Jesse W. Markham

THE

American

Political

Process

EDITED BY

Leonard W. Levy and John P. Roche

George Braziller   NEW YORK   1963

To Our Children

JOANNA RATCLIFF ROCHE

WENDY ELLEN LEVY   LESLIE ANNE LEVY

ACKNOWLEDGMENTS

The American Political Science Association generously gave permission to reprint materials for which it holds the copyright. We are grateful for its cooperation. Mr. William Leiss, a doctoral candidate in the History of Ideas program at Brandeis University, performed invaluable services as a research assistant and critic. We are appreciative, too, of Mrs. Dorothy Roach's skillful secretarial work.

PREFACE

*I*N THE AUTUMN of 1961 Harvard University was asked to organize an orientation program for seventy-five Brazilian student leaders being sent to the United States by the Cultural Union of São Paulo and the Department of State. The Office of Latin American Studies at Harvard arranged for four of us, specialists in American studies, to work with these students during the ten days they were to be in Cambridge.

When we began to prepare the program, we discovered that there were no suitable texts either in Portuguese or English. Such books of readings as existed were designed for college courses or, at the very least, assumed some specialized knowledge on the part of the reader. While we could expect the Brazilian students to be intelligent and well-informed about Brazil, we had to assume that they would know almost nothing about how the United States had grown, what its culture was, or how its democracy or economic system worked. To meet their needs, we felt we should put together four entirely new volumes containing basic readings.

When the Brazilian students arrived, these volumes were not yet ready. The four of us circulated some of the readings among them. We also talked with them at length and tried to answer their questions and find out what about the United States interested and puzzled them.

We are not sure yet what effect our teaching may have had. Among those hostile to the United States, we did not look for conversion. What we hoped was merely that all of them would go home knowing more about America, unable any longer to voice oversimplifications, and to this extent we think we did succeed. In any event, we hope that these four volumes, with their introductions, will enable others to undertake similar ventures.

Unlike comparable works, these volumes are designed for readers who have no specialized background in these fields, and, because they were constructed with a foreign audience in mind, they introduce perspectives that may be interesting even to specialists. While foreign readers should find in them the profile of America, readers nearer home may get, as well, a sense of the American image.

In this volume, Professors Levy and Roche have brought together readings that show government in the United States as it actually is. The first a historian whose works have reshaped his generation's ideas about the era of the Founding Fathers, the second a noted political scientist and popular writer and a leader of Americans for Democratic Action (national chairman since 1962), both have become aware from their researches and experiences that the true picture is not conveyed by such neat, static categories as federal—state—local, or executive—legislative—judicial. Using specific and easily understood examples from reports, commentaries, court decisions, messages, and even press conferences, they single out human conflict and co-operation as the reality, portray balances shifting almost from day to day, and also indicate how many problems the system has scarcely begun to solve. Here one sees in sharp outline the imagination and vigor, the willingness to experiment and compromise, the eagerness to meet challenges and cope with them, that have brought the United States to its present place and give it promise of a future no less rich and exciting than its past.

ERNEST R. MAY

CONTENTS

INTRODUCTION

Leonard W. Levy and John P. Roche

THE CONSTITUTION AND FEDERALISM

*T*HE LOGICAL POINT of departure for an examination of American government is obviously the Constitution of the United States. Yet the fundamental law of the Republic resembles Martin Chuzzlewit's grandnephew who had only "the first idea and sketchy notion of a face." A careful reading of the Constitution can only leave the inquirer puzzled: the short document is clear on structure, but at no point did the framers delineate power relationships with any precision. Obviously, by requiring the consent of two-thirds of Congress and three-quarters of the state legislatures to amend the Constitution, the draftsmen intended to curb the power of majorities. A Congress and President working together were denied the right to alter the constitutional framework without permission from a huge proportion of the states. Yet nowhere in the Constitution is the authority to restrain the national government explicitly conferred: neither the national judiciary nor the state governments were given any institutional mechanism to force the national government to conform to constitutional restrictions.

Indeed, a moment's reflection will suggest that had the Constitution been written in elaborate detail in 1787, it could never have survived the transformation of the United States from an underdeveloped, post-colonial nation with an agrarian base to an industrial, urban giant. In 1790, 95% of the American populace lived in communities of less than 2,500 inhabitants; there were only two "cities" with more than 25,000 people! According to the 1960 census, roughly 70% of the population lives in urban areas—and less than 10% of the work force is engaged in agriculture. But the same Constitution supplies the ground rules of national political life. What accounts for the durability of the document of 1787?

Surely not ease of amendment. The first ten amendments—the Bill of Rights—were added in 1791. Since then another thirteen have been incorporated, but of the latter only one—the fourteenth—has anything basic to say about the allocation of governmental power; it was the constitutional obituary of states' rights passed after the Civil War (1861-65). The twentieth-century amendments are constitutional trivialities which in no meaningful fashion altered the structure of power in the nation: two memorialized the classic and abortive effort to add "Thou Shalt Not Drink!" to fundamental law, one was a posthumous attack on President Franklin D. Roosevelt for winning the Presidency four times, one overruled an absurd judicial decision that the national government could not lay an effective income tax, several deal with electoral matters, and the most recent conferred the right to participate in Presidential elections upon the residents of the federal district. In short, only one amendment was concerned with a vital political relationship—that of states and nation. The viability of the Constitution must have its source in other considerations.

"A constitution," Chief Justice John Marshall observed in 1819, should not "contain an accurate detail of all the subdivisions of which its great powers will admit" nor "of all the means by which they may be carried into execution"; on the contrary, "Its nature . . . requires that only its great outlines should be marked, its important objects designated, and the minor ingredients which compose those objects be deduced from the nature of the objects themselves." Marshall was arguing, to put it another way, that it was precisely the lack of specificity, the ambiguity, which gave the Constitution its strength and adaptability. And American history has clearly sustained his view. There has been no need to amend the Constitution, or to rewrite it from time to time, because the original document could be interpreted anew by each generation in terms of its own problems.

Congress, for example, was granted (Article I, Section 8) jurisdiction over "commerce among the states." In the context of 1787, before the transportation revolution, this mainly amounted to maintaining a national market by preventing the states from establishing trade barriers among themselves and discriminating against each other's products. However, in *Gibbons v. Ogden*, the Supreme Court in 1824 explained that "interstate commerce" was far more than just goods in transit; it was the whole process of commercial intercourse between the states. When the burden of transportation was taken over by the railroads in the last quarter of the nineteenth century, the doctrine of *Gibbons v. Ogden* was applied to give Congress the authority to regulate the rates, safety practices, and financial procedures of interstate carriers and later of *intra*state railroads which "affected" interstate commerce. Furthermore, the commerce power was used by Congress to forbid the shipment over state lines of "bad" objects, such as lottery tickets, prostitutes, prize-fight films, stolen cars, and oil produced in violation of state law.

This expansion of the scope of interstate commerce did not take place without considerable stress and strain and occasional judicial fireworks (as, for example, when the Supreme Court held that Congress did not have the power to bar from interstate commerce goods made by child labor—*Hammer v. Dagenhart,* 1917), but despite ups and downs of constitutional interpretation, the history of the commerce clause is one of ever increasing scope. Although the courts had a hand in the matter, this expansion was fundamentally undertaken by the President and Congress—the so-called "political organs" of the national government—and was initially incorporated in great statutes such as the Interstate Commerce Act of 1887, the Transportation Act of 1920, the National Labor Relations Act of 1935, and the Fair Labor Standards Act of 1938. The role of the judiciary in the power structure of American national government will be discussed later; suffice it here to note that the courts inevitably deal with constitutional issues *a posteriori*—they have no power of initiative.

The nub of the matter is that today, despite the absence of any change in the wording of the commerce clause of the Constitution, there is no effective *constitutional* limitation on Congressional power over the national economy. It is impossible now to delineate between inter- and intrastate commerce on any firm legal basis. The federal minimum wage law *could* unquestionably be extended to cover all employees in the nation; the present large exclusions (agricultural

workers, laundry workers, etc.) are a consequence of political rather
than constitutional imperatives.

The same course of expanded development has been associated
with the taxing power: the constitutional grant to tax and spend for
"the General Welfare" (Article I, Section 8) has provided the
national government with a rationale for intervening in the affairs of
state and local governments. Cities, for example, can only qualify to
receive the great benefits of the federal program of urban renewal by
adopting certain standards established in Washington. Technically
speaking, cities are subordinate to state governments and in no direct
way subject to federal jurisdiction (Washington, D.C., of course,
excepted), but in this indirect fashion—by what opponents call
"bribery"—the national government intrudes its authority.

Keeping in mind, then, that at most essential points the United
States has an *unwritten* Constitution which is constantly being altered
to adapt to new governmental exigencies—and that the bulk of this
change is gradual and unchallenged—what can be said about the
character of American federalism?

The basis of federalism is the premise that in the United States
there is a division of sovereignty between the national government
and the states, with the former exercising "delegated" powers and
the latter retaining, or "reserving," all authority not delegated. In
ideal terms, this is simple stuff: just as two trains coming from oppo-
site directions pass each other uneventfully on a double track, so the
jurisdictions of the nation and of the states *should* not come into
conflict.

As medieval political theorists, laboring to delineate the proper
spheres of secular authority (*imperium*) and spiritual sovereignty
(*sacerdotium*), learned to their dismay, this type of model has one
great built-in problem: *Who* determines which is which? To put the
matter differently, it is possible to accept the legitimacy of state
power, to believe sincerely in states' rights, and yet to insist that the
national government, or an agency of the national government such
as the Supreme Court, has the authority to determine what the *content* of legitimate state powers shall be. And the converse can be

equally true: a strong nationalist such as James Madison could once assert that the states as well as the Court had the authority to determine when the general government had overstepped its proper bounds.

The federal system which emerged from the Constitutional Convention reflected a practical effort to build as strong a central government as political imperatives would permit against a background of existing state power. The crucial question of who was to referee conflicts of jurisdiction between the states and the nation was neatly begged in Article VI which provided that "This Constitution, and the Laws which shall be made in Pursuance thereof . . . shall be the Supreme Law of the Land" and thus binding on the states. While this "Supremacy Clause" seems to put the matter neatly, in fact it merely opened up for subsequent debate and decision the key question: who is to decide whether any piece of challenged legislation is, or is not, in "Pursuance" of the Constitution?

Space does not permit exploration of this fascinating historical issue except to note that final determination that the national government had the power to define its own authority vis-à-vis the states came only after Union victory in a bloody Civil War. Since that time the doctrine of states' rights has been invoked from time to time by the Supreme Court to curb the power of the national government (the last time was 1936), but it should be noted that an instrument of the national government, the high Court, did this *in behalf* of state authority. The view that there is inherent power in the states to resist "unconstitutional" invasions of state jurisdiction has no legal foundation, but—as the efforts of Southern state governments to resist school desegregation indicate—the concept of states' rights lives on in the political arena as a source of political slogans.

However, while federalism may be more a source of argument than a viable constitutional theory, it is also clear that an American state government does exercise great power and is in no sense comparable to a British urban borough or a French *département*. The average citizen is not interested in constitutional niceties and from his viewpoint the state government, or one of its subdivisions, educates his children, builds roads, defines his property rights (by zoning ordinances, for example), operates health and welfare programs, and arrests and prosecutes those who injure him or steal his silverware. In other words, while on the constitutional plane the states may have no significant protection from the inroads of the national government, they are in practice anything but legal dependencies of Washington. Although stripped of their constitutional defenses by the Civil War and by the whole modern development of the war, taxing, and commerce powers of the federal government, the states are hardly prone and defenseless. Indeed, the states have enormous *de facto* authority and only under conditions of unusual political stress does the states' rights issue even get raised.

The reason there is so little conflict between the jurisdictions is, to oversimplify, that the national government has quietly waived much of its power and jurisdiction to state authorities under the doctrine of "cooperative federalism." Every year, for example, hundreds of millions of dollars are distributed to state education departments under the federal "impacted area" program. This is federal aid to compensate the states for the special problems created by national activities, *e.g.*, the burden on local education growing out of the existence of a huge, tax-exempt federal installation—military post, Atomic Energy Commission laboratory, etc.—within a school district. In similar fashion, the federal Civil Defense program contributes to the purchase of local fire apparatus; grants-in-aid are made for maternal services, road-building, school lunches, crippled children, vocational rehabilitation, and dozens of other programs; and the United States puts up two-thirds of the funds for urban renewal. Except when racial or religious issues get involved (school desegregation and the question of subvention of private religious educational institutions have been recent sources of ideological tension), the state governments are delighted to accept and administer this largesse and are quite prepared to let sleeping states' rights dogmas lie.

But *why* does the federal government thus devolve its sovereignty? Now we reach the heart of the matter: in the United States the states are the effective units of *political organization*. The nation does not in any meaningful sense of the concept have a two-party system, one in which two disciplined national parties confront each other in every polling place. For Presidential purposes, every four years a Democratic candidate opposes a Republican, and behind each nominee the state parties which carry the Democratic or Republican banner uniformly (but not inevitably) coalesce. (In 1960 the Mississippi Democrats refused even to put John F. Kennedy's name on the ballot, and in both 1952 and 1956 the Democratic organization in Virginia effectively supported Dwight Eisenhower. Also in 1960 several state Democratic parties in the South repudiated the national Democratic Platform!) These two nationwide coalitions of state parties fight out the Presidential election, but once the White House is occupied for another term, politics reverts to the state level—and to Congress, which is chosen on a state and local constituency basis. The President, whether Democratic or Republican, finds himself a national political figure without any significant national political machinery: the national committees of the parties have no policy functions, but spend their time between Presidential contests raising money to pay debts. (Exact figures are hard to find, but it is estimated that each party in 1960 spent over $15,000,000 in contesting the Presidency and that *all* election costs came to $160,000,000!)

As will be noted in the next section, leading Congressmen of both parties have always taken a dim view of the possibility of national, organized party machinery. These men, who have achieved committee chairmanships in the House and Senate by accumulating seniority, *i.e.*, by returning for term after term from politically non-competitive constituencies, consider any attempt at national party organization as an instrument of Presidential aggrandizement. In the absence of any countervailing power, these magnates can deal with the President from positions of unchallenged strength and they have no interest in strengthening the Chief Executive's hand. To take a recent example, a nationally structured Democratic Party would obviously be based on the cities and would have vigorously endorsed President Kennedy's effort in 1962 to create an executive Department of Urban Affairs. However, the Republicans and Southern Democrats in the

House combined to kill the proposal and met no organized opposition. All the President could do was castigate them at a press conference; he was trapped in a political vacuum.

If the development of strong national parties is in the Presidential interest, the maintenance of state and local authority is the continuing goal of Congressional committee chairmen and their senior opponents in the minority. For one thing, power in state governments is notoriously rigged against the cities: legislative districts are designed to give the city voters the least possible say in state governments, and there are often gross mathematical disparities between the population of urban and of rural districts: it is not uncommon to have one rural vote weigh as much in the selection process as three city votes. (In 1962 the Supreme Court virtually ruled that such population disparities violated the Fourteenth Amendment's equal protection clause, but it will be some time before the impact of this decision will really be felt.)

Thus if it comes to a Congressional choice between giving a major task to the federal government to be administered directly or delegating the matter to the states, the powerful Congressmen in both houses will immediately opt for the state solution—even if it is manifestly inefficient and cumbersome, as is the case with unemployment compensation. This is not just an ideological preference; it is founded on hard political facts. The Congressman is directly tied to his local party organization—state, county, or city—and these bodies have a tremendous vested interest in state government (which, of course, includes county and municipal governments). Local political machines live on patronage—on jobs, contracts, favors—and state and local governments are a prime source of this political lubricant. While about 95% of all federal jobs are under civil service (which does not necessarily eliminate patronage entirely), the fundamental motto of state and local government is still "To the Victors belong the Spoils." (It is hard to be exact in these matters, but experts are in agreement that county government is the greatest locus of corruption in the United States.)

The state governments then not only survive, but flourish as the base of operations of parochialism in American politics. To take a concrete example, the federal government could certainly undertake a huge road-building program on its own authority under the commerce power, the war power, the post-road power, or a combination of all three. Under these circumstances the Director of the Bureau of Roads would have billions of dollars worth of contracts to allocate and he could, if he were so motivated, probably line up every contractor in the United States behind the President. No one, of course, would bring any pressure on the contractors to support the President, but one can predict a spontaneous opening of hearts—and pocketbooks—in support of his policies. These contractors might, for example, subsidize the campaigns of candidates selected by the President in local areas.

This would clearly be a violation of states' rights—or so it would be proclaimed by all statesmen in the House and Senate. To avert Presidential "dictatorship," they would recommend and pass a system (such as the one currently in operation) where the federal government simply provides the bulk of the funds for road-building but leaves the allocation of contracts, and the cultivation of contractors, to the proper state authorities. This is a highly practical and realistic approach to political theory by men who are convinced that the growth of centralized Presidential power is a threat to traditional American institutions. They are prepared to accept the fact that in the sixth decade of the twentieth century the functions of the national government must be expanded, but they want to adjust the Constitution to the exigencies of the age in such a way as to retain the diffused power structure characteristic of an earlier less complicated epoch.

To conclude, American federalism has lost its theoretical base; since 1937, the constitutional doctrine of states' rights has lost all standing and is now an exhibit in the museum of judicial curiosities. However, at the same time, the balance between states and nation has been roughly maintained through the operations of a political party system based on state organizations which has a vested interest in sustaining the operational—if not theoretical—prerogatives of state governments. The states are therefore very much in business whatever may be their abstract juridical status and serve as vital governmental entities in "copartnership" with the national government.

THE SEPARATION OF POWERS

To turn from the relationships between the states and the nation to the interrelationships within the federal government is comparable to moving from a large-scale map to an enlarged insert. Just as the lines of demarcation between the nation and the states were left imprecise in the Constitution, so the jurisdictions of the President, the Congress and the federal judiciary were ambiguously defined. In essence, the Constitution created these three governmental bodies and left to them the task of defining their own areas of authority. Thus the cliché that the United States government is based on the "separation of powers" is at best half-true; in fact powers are blended, not separated. The so-called "independence" of the American President arises from his fixed four-year term and his election by a distinctive constituency—the people as a whole, not from any body of formal powers that he can exercise. To put it differently, the President of the United States is an enormously powerful figure—he stands as the spokesman for the nation in foreign affairs, initiates legislation, commands the defense establishment, and supervises the execution of national policy—but his authority is more a function of his political pre-eminence than of his arsenal of constitutional weapons.

For example, the least restricted of the President's powers is his authority as Commander-in-Chief of the armed forces: in this capacity he can effectively commit the United States to warlike measures without consulting Congress—though the latter is charged with the decision on war by the Constitution. As Commander-in-Chief, President Truman in June, 1950, ordered American troops to the aid of South Korea, and Congress subsequently endorsed his action. However, the Republicans, and some Democrats, in Congress disliked Truman's exercise of authority, and within a year the Democratic

Administration was being attacked—the Democrats, said leading Republicans, were the American "War Party." Disgust with the Korean War became widespread and was utilized very effectively by Republican strategists in the 1952 Presidential campaign.

The lesson was learned by both Democrats and Republicans: in 1954, when the French were toppling in Indo-China, Vice-President Nixon and others urged immediate commitment of American forces on the Truman pattern to redress the balance, but the President and his political advisers killed the project. Whatever might be the President's constitutional authority, they did not want to get into an exposed political position where they could be attacked as a "War Party." Indeed, President Eisenhower went to great lengths to obtain from Congress advanced authorization for any actions he might deem necessary in the Formosa Straits and in the Middle East, and Congress responded with resolutions to this effect. The Kennedy Administration's great caution in dealing with the crises in Laos and Viet Nam—particularly the elaborate euphemisms which were employed in early 1962 to explain that American soldiers in those parts might be shooting but were not making war—was based on the same hard political calculation: the Democrats were not again going to be tagged as the "War Party."

In another sector of political life, the President has, at least according to the standard organizational charts, authority over executive departments and the national administration generally. However, in fact he is caught between civil service, which provides extensive job security for office-holders in the second and lower echelons of government, and the requirement that all top appointments be approved by the Senate. Thus, on the one hand, there are few administrative officials who can be summarily removed by a new President, and, on the other, important positions can only be filled with the consent of the Senate. When one adds to this the consideration that members of such vital regulatory agencies as the Federal Reserve Board, the Interstate Commerce Commission, the Securities and Exchange Commission, the Federal Communications Commission (to mention only a handful of the so-called "independent regulatory commissions") are appointed for stipulated terms (14 years in the case of the Reserve Board) which overlap Presidencies, and are virtually unremovable, the difficulties of the President in achieving policy control over "his" administration can be appreciated.

Although the Senate intrudes on executive power through its oversight of appointments (which is seldom exercised because wise Presidents clear their nominees in advance of formal nomination with Senatorial magnates), the President is also endowed by the Constitution with a formidable chunk of "legislative" power: the veto. In net terms, the President has the same legislative authority as two-thirds of both houses of Congress—the vote required to override a veto. Moreover, the existence of the veto power makes its frequent use unnecessary; an advance intimation to Congress that certain measures will be vetoed usually leads to legislative alterations, particularly in important bills. And, although there is no constitutional basis for the practice, the President today initiates, through his party spokesmen in Congress, all important legislative proposals.

The really crucial matter which lies at the root of all governmental relationships is, of course, the power of the purse. A President may have the finest policy aspirations imaginable, but they will not amount to much in practical terms unless he can get Congress to appropriate the requisite funds. It is not generally realized, for example, that one of the major difficulties in getting effective federal action under the various civil rights statutes is a consequence of persistent Congressional refusal to provide adequate staff for the Civil Rights Division of the Department of Justice. (In 1962 there were 271 lawyers staffing the Anti-Trust Division of the Department, but only 40 in Civil Rights.) Budgeting is done on an annual basis, and Congress generally insists that all appropriations must also be voted from year to year.

This often leads to confusion. Congress, at the behest of its committees on foreign policy (House Committee on Foreign Affairs, Senate Committee on Foreign Relations) and the President, may pass a comprehensive plan such as the Alliance for Progress, designed to allocate 20 billion dollars over a decade to Latin American economic and social development; but this is only the preamble to action. There is no money attached to such a ringing declaration; financing must be separately negotiated with different Congressional committees, the appropriations committees, and in separate legislative action approved by both houses. In the case of the Alliance for Progress, Congress sternly refused the President the authority to engage in "backdoor financing," *i.e.*, borrowing the necessary funds from the Treasury, despite the argument that this would provide necessary flexibility within an over-all long-term Congressional authorization. Consequently, the President must return to Congress annually to get the funds, and foreign statesmen are often left wondering whether, for example, a Presidential commitment to give aid over a five-year period will be matched by annual Congressional appropriations over the same period. Congress has been quite responsible about meeting Presidential commitments—most of the worrying in Brasilia or London, Paris or New Delhi, has been unnecessary—but its latent power helps to keep the President extremely courteous and considerate toward the national legislature.

The meaningless character of most generalizations about the "separation of powers" becomes most apparent when one examines the operation of the federal administration. When the Republic was established, the administrative needs of the national government were met by a small bureaucracy—Secretary of State Thomas Jefferson presided over a staff in Philadelphia of roughly half a dozen—and the scope of national activities was very slight. Over the last half-century, and notably since the United States became involved in the first World War and a decade later the Great Depression, there has been an astronomical increase in both the size and jurisdiction of the federal bureaucracy. In addition to such great line agencies as the Treasury, the Department of Agriculture, or the Department of Health, Education, and Welfare, the bureaucratic map is spotted with various specialized organizations, among them the regulatory commissions referred to above. Excluding those in military service, there are approximately 2,500,000 federal employees—though, of course, they are not all in Washington but are scattered throughout the country.

What is important is not the number of agencies, but the general position of the bureaucracy in the federal government's power system. In theory, the President is "Chief Administrator," but—as one might suspect by now—in practice administrative politics consists of a grueling, perpetual struggle between the President and the Congress for control of bureaucratic decision-making. To begin with a fairly simple point, the power of the President to reorganize the national administration is exercised only with the approval of Congress: the executive must submit his reorganization plans to Congress and *either* house can block them by majority vote. (This is what occurred when the House defeated Kennedy's plan to establish a Department of Urban Affairs.) In similar fashion, either house may overrule a decision by the Attorney General to suspend the deportation of an alien, and in certain special categories (mainly subversive aliens) the Attorney General can suspend deportation *only* if both houses, by concurrent resolution, approve.

Other statutes require the involvement of Congressional committees before administrative action is taken. For instance, a suspicious Congress in 1944 required that contracts for the exploitation of Navy petroleum reserves should not be made "without prior consultation . . . with the Naval Affairs Committees of the Congress," and in 1952 Congress, in providing $1,200,000,000 for secret military construction, provided that the official involved "shall come into agreement with the Committee on Armed Services of the Senate and of the House of Representatives with respect to the cost of construction." Perhaps the high point in this Congressional intervention was the 1952 act which gave certain authority to the Director of the Bureau of the Budget contingent upon "the approval of the chairman of the Committee on Appropriations of the House of Representatives." In January, 1963, President Kennedy informed the Director of the Bureau of the Budget that such a "veto" provision was an unconstitutional violation of the principle of the separation of powers. To this Congressman Otto Passman of Louisiana, chairman of the foreign-aid subcommittee of the House Appropriations Committee and a long-time critic of overseas spending, replied that he was "serving notice on the Administration right now that its ruling is going to be the most expensive interpretation ever made of a law passed by Congress" and that in the future his committee would establish limitations on spending "so hard they will make concrete look soft." It might be added that Passman comes from a district where the Republicans do not even bother to run a candidate and he has no problems in the Democratic primary—as far as being influenced by national opinion is concerned, he might just as well be from Central Asia.

A final example indicates this interweaving of jurisdictions in its full glory. Under the trade agreement statutes, the Federal Tariff Commission, an independent regulatory body, is charged with the task of determining when a reduction in import duty will do "serious injury" to a domestic industry. After conducting an investigation, the Commission can report its views to the President and perhaps recommend an increase in the tariff (as it has done 41 times since 1950). From 1951 to 1958 the President was required to inform Congress of his reasons for not accepting the Commission's recommendations, but in 1958 the rule was changed: since that date Congress can by a two-thirds vote in both Houses overrule the President's decision and implement the view of the Commission. (No Presidential determination has yet been challenged in this fashion.)

In essence, the federal administration is a huge locus of authority. Many agencies exercise legislative, executive, and judicial power: they make rules, enforce the rules, and adjudicate violations of the rules all under their own roof, a development which was never anticipated by the founders of the Republic. (The Securities and Exchange Commission, for example, establishes rules governing stock issues, polices the money market, and brings offenders to book. The Department of Agriculture exercises similar authority over the national system of crop limitation and farm price stabilization.) As this power-complex has grown, both Congress and the Presidents have sought to maintain their authority, and to prevent this Leviathan from falling into the hands of the other. As a consequence, administrators are constantly exposed to counter-pulls—from the executive on one hand and the Congressional committees on the other. Congress, as was suggested earlier, is constantly on the lookout to prevent the growth of a Presidential political machine and it takes little insight to realize what could be done if 2,500,000 federal employees became political sepoys of the President. Congress, however, forestalled such a mobilization: the Hatch Acts, ostensibly designed to eliminate political corruption, politically sterilized the federal bureaucracy. It is a federal offense for federal employees (with certain exemptions at the top level) to engage in partisan political activities. Moreover, key Congressmen (such as the Chairman of the House Agriculture Committee) make it clear to key administrators (such as the Director of the Production and Marketing Administration of the Department of Agriculture) that—in the words of the late Speaker, Sam Rayburn— the way to "get along" is to "go along." With Congress controlling the funds this message usually gets through.

By now one might be under the impression that the national government of the United States is a perpetual donnybrook—a form of institutionalized chaos—but nothing could be farther from the truth. Indeed, the conflict between President and Congress is conducted under a protocol (traditional, informal, but yet binding) as well-structured as an English Country Dance. A strong President, one who builds an effective constituency among the pressure groups and the people at large, soon establishes a *modus operandi* with Congress and negotiations take place on the basis of realistic appraisals of strength. President Kennedy, for example, made it clear in 1961-62 that he was not going to permit Representative Carl Vinson of Georgia, Chairman of the House Armed Services Committee and a magnate of long standing, to exercise his customary sovereignty over the Department of Defense. Vinson brought matters to a head by attempting to force the Department to proceed with the development of the B-70, a huge supersonic bomber, despite Secretary McNamara's decision that in the missile age this plane was an expensive archaism. After prolonged Congressional rumbling failed to unsettle the President, Vinson's position became quite exposed; in a fashion almost feudal, he then negotiated peace with Kennedy in the White House garden. In contrast, it appeared that President Kennedy reached tacit agreement with leading Southerners in Congress that he would not confront them with vigorous demands for civil rights legislation so long as they did not sabotage his efforts to cope with the problem by judicial and administrative action.

A strong President, such as Theodore Roosevelt, Franklin D. Roosevelt, or John F. Kennedy, thus establishes a far different set of boundaries between executive and legislative power than a weak Chief Executive. Furthermore, the process of definition is perpetually underway and may lead to different equilibria in various areas of policy: every President since Franklin D. Roosevelt has run into a stone wall in the agricultural sector; Eisenhower and Kennedy have suffered far less attrition in foreign relations than Truman; and Kennedy has for the first time established a really integrated Department of Defense and brought the various competing armed services to heel. In juridical terms the powers of the Presidency have not been altered in a hundred and seventy years, but each President must work out his own power relationships in terms of his conception of the office and the strength of his national appeal; to a considerable extent the Greek maxim still stands as a fundamental insight into Presidential power: *character is fate*.

THE JUDICIARY AND CIVIL RIGHTS

The federal judiciary has a unique role in American government, one which merits special treatment in any analysis of power relationships. Not only do the judges, as was indicated earlier, play a vital role in defining the position of boundary lines between state and national jurisdiction, but they also intervene from time to time in the balance between President and Congress and, finally, act as arbiters in conflicts between individual citizens and the sovereign on both national and state levels. In addition to these political functions, the judiciary also adjudicates a huge mass of litigation arising from federal law and from diversity jurisdiction, *i.e.*, suits between citizens of different states where the amount at issue is more than $10,000. We are here concerned only with the political activities of the federal courts, such as the desegregation or reapportionment decisions which bring judicial authority to bear on the political sector.

The federal judiciary, in short, is very much "in politics" on the basic level—though on the superficial partisan level judges eschew party roles. They are not disembodied voices for the law to speak through, but men whose convictions can play an important part in determinations of public policy. This is recognized on all sides when judicial appointments are made: in 1961-2 President Kennedy had the opportunity to appoint over a hundred judges and only two Republicans made the grade. No President will ever forget the fearful slaughter that Republican judges wrought on Franklin D. Roosevelt's New Deal in the 1930's; indeed, from 1958 to 1961, a Democratic Congress held off authorizing badly needed judicial expansion on the presumption that a Democrat would win in 1960. The bet paid off.

It would be a mistake to think that most of the work of the federal courts is concerned with matters of high policy; the bulk of a judge's docket is taken up with routine litigation. But the power to intrude on policy-making is always lurking in the background and a District Judge who has spent his life on the bench coping with constitutionally trivial litigation may suddenly find himself engaged in a ferocious legal brawl with a state legislature over school desegregation, legislative apportionment, or the scope of state authority over interstate commerce. This latent power—which is virtually unknown in the judicial systems of other democratic nations—is an outgrowth of two main considerations: first, the essential ambiguity of the Constitution as to the boundaries between states and nation, and between the executive, legislative, and judicial jurisdictions of the national government; and, second, the absence of strong, national political parties which could provide the sort of disciplined Congressional majority (as in Great Britain) that would tolerate no judicial meddling in policy matters. In other words, it is the fluidity and diffusion of political power, discussed earlier, which provides the judges with their room for maneuver.

Let us examine as a case in point the Supreme Court decision on apportionment of state legislatures (*Baker v. Carr*) which turned the political universe topsy-turvy in 1962. For at least a century the urban areas of the country (and more recently the suburbs) have suffered under the domination of legislatures based largely on the rural areas. When the cities arose and became the centers of industrial development, the dominant forces in the state legislatures simply refused to allocate to them their proper share of representatives. The result was that no matter how large the urban sector of a state became, it could not gain control of the legislature: it was impossible to use a depreciated vote to obtain a proportionate voice. Moreover, Congress —affected by the same skewing towards the rural areas—was unwilling and possibly powerless to remedy the problem. (The constitutional validity of Congressional action was obscure: the Fourteenth Amendment forbade any state to deprive persons within its jurisdiction of the equal protection of the laws and authorized Congress to implement this mandate. No effort has even been made in Congress to apply this provision to state apportionment legislation, though one could clearly argue that a statute which makes one man's vote the equivalent of those of three men in another district—or one to three hundred in Georgia—denies the equal protection of the laws. Indeed, in 1962 a federal circuit court, following *Baker v. Carr*, held this to be the case.)

Since the state legislatures and the Congress expressed no interest in remedying this distortion of the "will of the people" (despite the bitter complaints of the underrepresented), the issue, like racial segregation, arrived on the judicial agenda. Note that in political terms the Supreme Court was at a balance point between two constituencies: either way it decided the case, it stood to gain important and powerful champions. If it maintained precedent and ruled that state apportionment was not a matter for judicial evaluation, the Court would retain the support of those who favored the rural *status quo*. If it overruled or "distinguished" precedent and held that the

Fourteenth Amendment required equitable apportionment, it would become a heroic body in the eyes of the urban majority—both Democrats and Republicans. To put the matter in cold power terms, the Court had nothing to lose either way. In any event, the Justices invoked the equal protection clause and made possible the destruction of a legislative way of life.

In contrast, the freedom of maneuver of the federal judiciary is severely limited when a high level of national consensus exists on an issue. This is notably the case in wartime when it is virtually inconceivable that the Supreme Court would invalidate an important piece of defense or internal security legislation. It is not that the Justices consciously check the barometer of public opinion and calculate, but rather that as politicians they tend to make an automatic adaption to an environment and act accordingly. (They seem notably responsive to Congressional opinion: even during the New Deal period measures with a high degree of *bipartisan* support seldom ran onto judicial shoals.) Thus William O. Douglas and Hugo Black, who have built up a libertarian reputation over the past fifteen years, were notable supporters of the limitation of civil rights during World War II. In fact, it was Black who wrote the opinion of the Court (*Korematsu v. United States*, 1945) validating the arrest and detention in concentration camps of 75,000 American citizens for the crime of possessing Japanese ancestors. But rarely except in wartime does the level of national agreement on any given issue approach unanimity; even under the stresses of the Cold War, there have been widespread and vociferous differences of opinion on the techniques and principles of coping with Communist subversion or potential subversion.

American opinion is nowhere near as monolithic as the critics of our "conformist" society would have it. As evidence for this, one might suggest that there has developed in the United States over the past thirty years a strong tradition of civil rights, a tradition which has, despite the aberrations of the McCarthy period, flourished since the end of World War II. The incredible breakthrough of the Negro toward his rightful station as a full participant in American life has been the outstanding recent development, but judged by the standards of the past even the Communist today has rights which were unknown to political deviants in the first quarter of the twentieth century. A Communist leader seems to spend most of his time litigating his rights; an I.W.W. militant fifty years ago was fortunate if he ever got to the courtroom alive, and any trial he received was likely to be a camouflaged lynching. It was not until 1931 that the Supreme Court (*Near v. Minnesota*) declared a state action limiting civil rights (freedom of the press in this instance) violative of the Constitution.

Without going into historical detail, it is now the case that the federal courts impose a high level of procedural standards on both state and national governments. With regard to the national government, the explicit procedural requirements of the Bill of Rights (the first ten amendments to the Constitution) are enforced: no one can be convicted of a felony in a federal court without both indictment by grand jury and trial by petit jury (where a unanimous decision of the twelve members is required); the United States cannot introduce in evidence materials obtained by "unreasonable search and seizure" (and for a different reason it cannot employ recordings obtained by wire tapping); the defendant must be defended by counsel; he cannot be forced to incriminate himself; and so on. The defendant is innocent until proven guilty, and the judge must instruct the jury that a verdict of *not guilty* is mandatory unless they are convinced "beyond a reasonable doubt" of culpability. It is a fair generalization that no other nation in the world puts such elaborate restraints upon its law enforcement machinery. (It would be difficult to find in the records of any other state a decision comparable to the one a decade ago which prevented prosecution of an alleged Soviet espionage agent because the United States was barred from introducing in evidence crucial data obtained by wire taps. The Federal Bureau of Investigation understandably has some difficulty understanding the accusation that the United States is a "police state.")

The formidable restraints on the federal government operate with somewhat less force upon the states. Here the Supreme Court has ruled that an individual must, under the obligations of the due process clause of the Fourteenth Amendment, receive a "fair trial." However, the Justices have refused to define precisely the components of a fair trial and have permitted the states considerable procedural latitude. While the Court has ruled that anyone under indictment for a capital offense must have the assistance of counsel, it has not made this a mandatory requirement in all felonies but rather examines individual convictions on appeal to determine whether the denial of counsel has resulted in an unfair trial. States may abolish the grand jury and, indeed, alter the size and voting procedures in the petit jury. Moreover, neither the federal privilege against self-incrimination nor the federal bar on double jeopardy are fully operative vis-à-vis the states—though it is probable that the Court would hold extreme instances of either to be a denial of fair trial. In 1961, by contrast, the Court applied the full federal rule on unreasonable search and seizure to the states: evidence unreasonably obtained (for example, without a search warrant) is now inadmissible in both federal *and* state jurisdictions.

While the federal judiciary, and particularly the Supreme Court (to which come appeals from state decisions), thus play a vital role in defending the citizen's rights, it would be erroneous to suggest that the courts alone have a hand in the maintenance of civil liberty. The President has great potential power in this area through legal and administrative action. President Truman, for example, with one stroke of his pen ended racial segregation in the United States armed forces and at military bases and other facilities. He also instituted administrative measures to bar racial discrimination by government contractors—the first major Southern industries to desegregate their work forces were those who received contracts from the Atomic Energy Commission. President Eisenhower (who as Chief of Staff of the Army had opposed Truman's desegregation order) added little initiative, but under the Kennedy Administration the Attorney General, Robert Kennedy, threw the full force of the Department of Justice into the struggle for racial equality with notable results. And in 1962 President Kennedy struck a body blow to residential

discrimination by forbidding the use of federal funds to build, or aid in the building of, segregated housing.

Finally, though the power of Southern magnates obviously makes it a difficult accomplishment, Congress has passed some civil rights legislation. A 1960 statute (passed after a solid week of round-the-clock Southern filibustering in the Senate) strengthened considerably the authority of the federal government to prevent disfranchisement of Negroes and provided the legal basis for the numerous right-to-vote suits subsequently instituted by Attorney General Kennedy.

In summary then, a democratic idealist can quite properly criticize the United States for falling short of its high ideals in the realm of equality and human freedom. But at the same time, as an inhabitant of a contingent universe, he should also concede that tremendous strides have been taken toward fulfilling the imperatives of the American dream and that by comparison with most other free societies (to say nothing of the unfree) the American citizen is armed with a remarkable arsenal of rights against his sovereigns. (If American police practices leave a great deal to be desired, they are clearly Utopian when compared, for example, with the brutal ruthlessness of French *gendarmes*.) And while these rights are founded in the first analysis on the Constitution, they rest on the sense of decency and fair play of the people as a whole. Perhaps it is worth noting that at the height of the anti-Soviet frenzy—in the late 1940's when Stalin had made clear his aggressive designs—the General Secretary of the American Communist Party (who had publicly announced his loyalty to the Soviet Union) was excused from standing trial for sedition because he was suffering from heart trouble.

CONCLUSION

The picture of American government that has emerged here is quite different from that conveyed by the study of organizational charts. While one can isolate a number of different political forces on the American scene—state governments, parties, pressure groups, courts, Congressmen, Presidents, and administrators are highly visible

entities—constantly shifting equilibria, changing coalitions, have made it extremely difficult to provide a set of static definitions. An enormous amount of power is "up for grabs," and its ultimate diffusion is a consequence of the strength of the various competitors. President Kennedy's successful counteroffensive against the steel companies in April, 1962, was a fine example of the process of definition in action. When the great steel firms raised their prices, they were quite within their legal rights; yet when the Chief Executive denounced them for betraying the national interest and marshaled a formidable combination of moral pressure and legal and economic sanctions (the Attorney General began a vociferous investigation of alleged collusion, the Secretary of Defense awarded a big contract to a firm which had *not* raised its prices, etc.), these giants of American capitalism collapsed like tents in a tornado. When the industrialists rescinded their price increase, it was clear that Kennedy had successfully invoked the prestige of his office in a fashion unknown to any of his predecessors.

Now, to the great alarm of the business community and so-called "conservatives," this will become a "precedent" and be cited in all books on the powers of the President. But if any future President thinks that he can pull off the same feat simply because in his manual of powers there is a footnote to the steel price rollback, he will be sadly mistaken. As President Truman learned to his fury in 1952, every Chief Executive has to make his own way in a hostile world; while Franklin D. Roosevelt had seized industries when he felt their wartime conduct was undermining national security, and the courts had remained in judicious hibernation, Truman's action in seizing the steel mills when production stopped during the Korean War was declared unconstitutional by the Supreme Court. At the same time, the high Court did not absolutely foreclose seizure in a national emergency; it left the future to work this problem out for itself by simply agreeing that Truman's emergency was not a *real* emergency. Thus in a real emergency the President's hands are not fettered, but the definition of a real emergency is something that has to be worked out in terms of the exigencies of any given situation, *i.e.*, to return to

the point under discussion, by the configuration of forces involved in the actual dispute.

Therefore, in the same way that a film is made up of a series of discrete still-shots but only makes sense when run through a motion picture projector, the institutions which are fixed points of American government must be seen in their interrelationships if one is to understand the political process. In a sense, the very act of analysis causes problems: the biology student can perform an elaborate dissection of the components of a frog, but the frog is dead and the sum total of characteristics of a dead frog do not add up to a description of a live frog. In the short compass of this essay, there has been little room for anatomical detail, and every effort has been made to describe the operating entity which is American government; the necessary and proper quest for specific institutional data can be satisfied easily by the *Congressional Directory* and any standard text.

There is one final point that needs some elaboration. What is on the surface a curiously chaotic system of government seems to work in a quite respectable fashion. Indeed, a pragmatic case can be made, on the basis of what we know of the operations of the Nazi state and on Khrushchev's observations to the 20th and 22d Party Congresses of the Soviet Union on the vagaries of Stalinist dictatorship, that the government of the United States is *at least* less inefficient than those that have boasted of their monolithic efficiency. (The definition of "efficiency" is elusive. Is a society that preserves freedom, even if it wastes time, energy and resources at a prodigious rate, an "inefficient" one?) How does the United States with its archaic Constitution, designed for a rural agrarian age, and its fluid, even atomistic, political system get anything accomplished?

Here we arrive at the fundamental level of political reality, that fundamental agreement on goals and ideals which is the bedrock of American institutions. This consensus is virtually impossible to explain in wholly rationalistic terms. On one hand, there is ample room in American society for ferocious disagreements on matters of political, social, and economic policy; on the other, there is, whether through habit, or conviction, or a combination of both, a set of basic ideals about *the way* the community solves its problems. As in any society, there are those who reject these ground rules (*e.g.*, fanatical racists, Communists, Birch Society militants), but the history of the past half century has shown a steady decline in the political power of these alienated and destructive groups. The Democratic National Convention of 1924 refused to condemn the Ku Klux Klan!

Every society sets limits on deviation, and the United States is no exception. The "open society," one in which there are no limits, is a logical chimera—and would probably be a shambles, if it were conceivable. What distinguishes a democratic community from its authoritarian or totalitarian counterpart is not its commitment to "total freedom" (whatever that might be), but the criteria and the techniques by which the limits of acceptable behavior are established. A democratic society obviously has a vital stake in maintaining those values which alone can make the accomplishment of freedom a reality; it is, in the phrase of the late Justice Jackson, no suicide pact. At the same time, the techniques of limiting dissent can pose a threat to the principles these actions are allegedly preserving; suppression is a contagious disease in politics.

There is no theoretical answer to this problem. In practical terms, the outer limit of consensus is the imminent threat of the firing squad. The dissenter is left alone by the law until he presents a "clear and present danger" to the fundamental values of the community. The leaders of a free society are under no obligation to welcome their executioners; ideally they will not institute repressive legal action unless there is a real potential threat to the survival of the society, and they will distinguish between fierce verbal and written threats and the existence of a trained, disciplined and dangerous conspiracy aiming at the concrete seizure of power. (Thus, in realistic terms, despite the soundness of the logic involved, the suppression of the American Communist Party for its undeniable aspiration to overthrow the government of the United States can hardly be pragmatically justified: it is the Soviet Union and its espionage agents, who presumably do not "surface" at the Communist rallies, not the Communist Party, that threatens American survival.)

But leaving aside the problem of American Communists—who, by the way, had endless days in court, and stumped the country while on bail raising funds for their defense—and the nasty but politically insignificant extremists of the far right, there is a wide range of dissent without any threat of repression. To take a case in point, Senator Barry Goldwater, a militant conservative, disagrees strongly with the Kennedy Administration on most serious issues, and a vigorous liberal such as Senator Hubert Humphrey stood at the other end of the spectrum from the Eisenhower Administration. Yet, despite their often bitter disagreements, both men are within the consensus: each knows that a victory by the other will not lead to his execution. Neither lives out his political life in the shadow of the gallows; nor do socialists, pacifists, anarchists, or members of other dissenting minorities. Political life is wide open, even for advocates of gallows-politics, up to the point where the society determines by *judicial action* (not secret arrest and administrative imprisonment) that a group does constitute a real menace to the *modus vivendi*, to the tumultuous but still consensual way in which social decisions are reached. No individual or group, in other words, can be permitted to throw a spanner into the mechanism of choice and, in the name of History or whatever ideology, set up the gallows or the firing squad as the mechanism to dispose of "wrong" opinions, *i.e.*, of all political competition. Those who look at this proposition abstractly and assert that it rests on a logical contradiction should turn from logic to life and ask themselves whether the vigorous suppression of Naziism by the Prussian Police, in, say, 1931 would have been an "undemocratic" action.

There is, in short, a qualitative distinction between opponents who accept the ground rules of democratic decision-making and those who seek power only to destroy the democratic apparatus and replace it with a self-sanctified dictatorship. Fortunately in a stable democratic society such as Great Britain or the United States the bulk of the population falls into the former category and, since living in freedom involves a willingness to take risks (to risk "inefficiency," for example), the anti-democratic minorities—whatever their dreams of glory—can be legally ignored on the pragmatic ground that they are politically impotent. Logic must be tempered with common sense and there is no substitute for courage.

I.   The Governments of the United States

THE AMERICAN FEDERAL SYSTEM:

AN HISTORICAL SUMMARY

When the Constitution was ratified, there were men of little faith who believed with some justification that the new government would not —could not—long survive. Indeed, that the United States did not become Balkanized defied history; so vast a land of such heterogeneity in its population had never before been governed on principles of freedom. But the viability of the federal system had not been reckoned with. Federalism, one of the great contributions to the art of representative government, accommodated the American need for unity and effective national government without succumbing to uniformity or abandoning local freedom of action. The selection that follows, from the report of The Commission on Intergovernmental Relations, succinctly reviews the evolution and vicissitudes of the American federal system.

The Problem of Federalism

THE PROPER division of labor and authority between the Nation and the States is the key to maintaining the federal nature of our system of government. The lines of division are not static. They have been controversial from the beginning of our life as an independent country. They remain so today. . . .

This system has characteristically been very flexible, leaving a great deal of room for argument and adjustment. The division of powers between the Nation and the States leaves substantial authority

The Commission in Intergovernmental Relations, *A Report to the President for Transmittal to the Congress* (Washington: G.P.O., 1955), pp. 9-34.

with each, but the use and relative importance of powers may shift. The Constitution cannot be formally amended by either level of government without the participation of the other, but interpretation and usage may expand or contract the powers at either level. The National Government deals with the people directly, but it may also utilize the States to reach them indirectly. The States can write and change their own constitutions, but they must meet minimum requirements of the National Constitution. The States are equal in legal status, but not in size, wealth, and influence. In all these essentials the federal relationship is adjustable, within limits. It is affected by controversies over what any government in the system should do, as well as by concepts of what no government should do. Historically, the invocation of States rights has sometimes been as much a sign of opposition to a specific National policy as of attachment to local action as such.

The Changing Environment of Federalism

A realistic view of the prospects for a continuing federal balance compels notice of the changes that have come over our society since 1787. The changes have been physical, technological, economic, cultural, intellectual, and political. Most obvious of the main trends affecting the federal system are those, accentuated in recent decades, that have led to a great expansion in the National Government and its activities, in the proportion of national income passing through the Treasury, and in the degree of attention focused on Washington. Less obvious but equally relevant is the very significant expansion of State and local governments in recent years.

POPULATION CHANGES

The most elementary fact is the growth in total population, now over forty times what it was in 1787. This has come about through large-scale immigration, a fairly high birth rate, and a rapidly declining death rate. The remarkable rise in longevity, which in a century has perhaps doubled the average life expectancy, has helped push the population figures up. Greater population density has resulted in the multiplication of governmental functions.

More significant in some respects than the numbers are the changes in composition—the submergence and later revival of the Indians, and the introduction and gradual dispersion of people of many races, creeds, and colors. No other major power in history, working under the conditions of a free society, has breathed a common loyalty into such a vast and varied mixture of peoples.

Ethnic groups sometimes accentuate the geographic diversities in the country, and thereby increase the justification for a decentralized system of government. On the other hand, such groups, usually in the minority nearly everywhere, are also sometimes targets of local discriminations. The protection of their basic rights has therefore on occasion been a ground for National action in matters otherwise left to the States.

EFFECTS OF INDUSTRIALIZATION

The growth of population has been accompanied by a continually rising standard of living, thanks mainly to the progress of science, technology, industrialization, and specialization. In the decline of the relative self-sufficiency that so conspicuously characterized the agricultural and handicraft economy of our forefathers lies a principal explanation of our demands, not only for more government services to supply what private enterprise does not provide, but also to regulate many of the complex relations among the individuals and groups of an industrial society.

These demands have affected the activities of all levels of government. It was when the great industrial enterprises of the latter part of the 19th century outgrew the jurisdictions of their home States that the era of National economic regulation was ushered in. The Interstate Commerce Act of 1887 and the Anti-Trust Act of 1890 showed the way. Next to the Fourteenth Amendment, the growth of

National economic regulation marked the most fundamental altera-
tion in the federal balance prior to World War I. The Federal Departments of Commerce and Labor found their origins in this movement. Seventy years of legislation have not exhausted the impulses
toward National regulation brought about by the dynamics of
industrialization.

Industrialization made the corporate form of business organization
indispensable and required large-scale capital investments, raw mate-
rial sources, and markets. The past 75 years have accordingly witnessed a huge growth in the number and size of corporations, the
provision of a vast and fluid money supply, the expansion of stock
exchanges and credit facilities, the rise of mass advertising, and the
development of natural resources and markets at home and abroad.
The States through general incorporation laws continue to issue and
regulate corporate charters; they charter and supervise many credit
institutions; they license occupations; their courts get the bulk of
commercial litigation; they regulate insurance and they prosecute
frauds. But the depression of the 1930's drove home the lesson that
the industrial economy is a national economy whose main instruments, whether of money, credit, prices, or labor relations, are often
beyond the effective reach of the States acting separately.

Industrialization has spurred, and in turn been stimulated by, research and invention. In this field it is hard to disentangle the contributions of private initiative and government policy. Corporations,
universities, and foundations have contributed to the achievements of
individual inventors and scientists. The patent laws lend encouragement. Tax policy may advance or retard technological progress. Governments maintain laboratories, collect and publish statistics and
other scientific data, and contract for research. In some areas, such as
nuclear physics, research is almost wholly government supported.

DILEMMA OF THE CITIES

Industrialization has made city dwellers or suburbanites out of
most Americans. In 1790, 19 people lived on farms for every one who

lived in a town. Today, the farm population is less than a sixth of the total, and 2 people out of 3 live in urban areas. Cities need water supply and sewage disposal, police and fire protection, zoning and building and sanitary codes, street paving and lighting, mass transportation and off-street parking, libraries, schools, parks, and the like. City governments are commonly expected to furnish many of these services and facilities and have grown correspondingly.

If local powers and jurisdictions were equal to these tasks, fewer problems might be pushed upward for solution. But the steady drift of the population to cities has run far ahead of the needed adjustments in municipal authority. Many metropolitan areas overrun State borders; State lines are apparently immutable; and cities have trouble consolidating with their suburbs. Meanwhile, city voters form the heavy battalions in Statewide and National elections, and can make their influence partially felt in that way even though they may be frustrated by outdated municipal boundaries or legislative districts at home. Urbanization has thus added to the scope and complexity of both State and National responsibilities.

AGRICULTURE AND NATURAL RESOURCES

For the 1 in 6 who still lives on a farm, an agricultural revolution has transformed life, too. Free schools and all-weather roads, mechanization and electrification, fertilizers and hybrid and purebred strains, have brought remarkable increases in productivity and changed both the farm and the farmer. With more cultivated land but fewer people working it than in 1900, farmers supply food for twice as large a total population at a far higher living standard. Subsistence farms are still numerous, but many farms are factories, and their proprietors are businessmen as well as farmers, with investments and records to keep. They provide a sharp contrast to the still surviving pattern of sharecropping agriculture. . . .

It is partly cause and partly consequence that the era of the agricultural revolution matches very closely the period of greatest expansion in the manifold programs of the Department of Agriculture.

Farmers use the National Government freely, and regard the Department as essential to their welfare. The network of agricultural experiment stations and county extension activities is one of the leading examples of National-State cooperation. . . .

CHANGES IN SOCIAL OUTLOOK

Changes in social outlook have accompanied the economic and technological. Many early Americans, for all their dislike of monarchy, held a definitely stratified view of society. This view was manifest in their preference for indirect election of the President and Senate, even at a time when property qualifications sharply limited the franchise for the direct election of the House of Representatives. It was this attitude that fixed a lowly social status for laborers, indentured servants, and apprentices. . . . By the end of the century, industrialization and immigration had formed a new and larger working class around the mines and mills and in the cities. Efforts to ameliorate the lot of these people through social legislation and education formed a staple of political controversy in the early 1900's. More recently, similar controversy has attended the progress of unionization, desegregation, and various welfare programs. These developments have involved shifting and expanding concepts of the general welfare with the net effect of adding to the responsibilities of government at all levels.

No aspect of this expanded role of government is more conspicuous in domestic policy than the enlarged public concern for social security and economic stabilization. For nearly two decades after the Federal Reserve System was established, the indirect credit controls it provided were the principal peacetime means of stabilizing the national economy to avoid the extremes of inflation and deflation. But since the depression of the 1930's, governments have experimented with a variety of direct as well as indirect measures to prevent or alleviate economic distress. In this field plainly the National Government alone has the sufficiently extended jurisdiction and necessary fiscal powers to take the lead and carry the main burden in a time of severe economic hardship; the States then have a support-ing role. Similarly the National Government has taken the responsi-bility for action to stabilize the economy in periods of inflation. All levels of government, however, owe each other full cooperation, mutual trust, and an opportunity to plan together programs designed to meet economic emergencies. The responsibility assumed by the National Government in the Employment Act of 1946 also leaves the States an important role. Some programs that are designed to provide economic security are managed exclusively by the States, such as general assistance. In others, such as old age assistance, em-ployment security, and vocational rehabilitation, cooperative arrange-ments in which both States and National Government participate are the rule.

These activities have been accompanied by a greatly expanded use of Federal grants-in-aid to the States. In principle, grants-in-aid are as old as the authorization of grants of school sections in each town-ship to local governments by the Congress of the Confederation in the Ordinance of 1785. Down to the time of the depression, however, their use had been confined largely to programs to help the farmer and, after World War I, to stimulate highway construction. These programs continue, but the major use of the grant-in-aid during the past two decades has been in programs established to provide social and economic security.

THE UNITED STATES IN WORLD AFFAIRS

Overshadowing all domestic occasions for governmental action to-day is the new position of the United States in world affairs. George Washington warned his countrymen to avoid permanent foreign al-liances: sound advice when they could not influence the outcome of events overseas, and could hope to escape involvement if they gave no provocation. Jefferson and Monroe thought it still good advice, and so it remained through the 19th century.

Economically and politically, we played for more than a century of our national life a relatively inactive role in international relations.

Before World War I our exports were chiefly agricultural commodities, and our imports were manufactured goods. As a debtor nation in the balance of international payments, the United States sent abroad immigrant remittances and interest and dividends to European investors. Now, as a creditor nation, military and economic assistance to other governments, together with private investments in foreign countries, loom large in the balance of payments that sustain American exports. A substantial share of our imports is made up of raw materials, and more and more of our exports are of finished goods. Not only agricultural exports, but also the level of employment in many domestic industries therefore depend importantly on the maintenance of dollar purchasing power abroad.

The familiar story of events from the Spanish-American War to the Korean invasion need not be retold here to make the point that we are at present a different country playing a different role in a different world. National defense, war, diplomacy, and foreign aid have been the province of the National Government from the beginning. It is a striking change in degree, responding to a change in need, that makes expenditures for these functions now exceed all other expenditures of all governments in this country put together.

It is a testimony to the durability and flexibility of our federal system that its basic pattern has survived almost a century and three-quarters of changes of the magnitude and variety that have been sketched here. It should be no cause for surprise that in the process of adaptation strong differences of opinion over constitutional doctrine and administrative practice have arisen.

Constitutional Doctrine and Practice

The structure of the new National Government established in 1789 reflected closely the intent of the framers of the Constitution, for the Federalists controlled the Congress during the first decade. Issues of National-State relations that had been fought out in the

Convention were re-opened, however, in the very first Congress. Anti-Federalists urged that the National Government should have little administrative machinery of its own, outside the realm of foreign affairs, and instead should use the State courts, the county tax collectors and law enforcement officials, and the State militia to serve its needs. The key vote in Congress in 1791, defeating the tax collector proposal, was close but decisive. The principle was confirmed that where the National Government had constitutional power it would act through its own agents. The division of power, in other words, would determine the division of labor.

This proposition was generally accepted, and in the main governed the administrative relations between the Nation and the States through the 19th century: the post office, the revenue services, and the United States district courts were National establishments. But the principle was never absolute. A major exception from the beginning was the States' control of elections. Minor ones followed. For example, when the first prisoner was convicted and sentenced by a Federal court under Federal law, there was no place to keep him but in a county jail.

The principle soon came to be subtly but significantly modified in another way that the framers could scarcely have foreseen. Senators were generally appointed by the State legislatures. After the rise of political parties, Senators found that in dealing with the President they could take advantage of their power over the confirmation of his appointments. The rule of senatorial courtesy developed, and with it the practice of making appointments to Federal posts outside Washington on the recommendations of the Senators immediately concerned, that is, on the basis of local party endorsements. Not through official State action, therefore, but through the medium of the party organizations that influenced State legislatures and Senators alike, the field establishments of the National Government were often brought under local control. Andrew Jackson learned to dominate much of the local party machinery and to turn it against his adversaries in the Senate. But often the local party influence prevailed.

Lincoln found in 1861 that he could not trust many of his subordinates in field offices, for they owed their places to influences arrayed on the Confederate side.

THE ISSUE OF NATIONAL SUPREMACY

The basic constitutional question for the federal system from 1789 to 1865 was the issue of National supremacy: whether the National Government was entitled to enforce, over State objections, decisions reached through its own constitutional processes. . . . The first open challenge after 1789 came in 1798 when Jefferson and Madison inspired the Virginia and Kentucky resolutions denouncing the alien and sedition acts. They invited the other State legislatures to instruct their Senators to vote for repeal of the acts, and went on to intimate that the States had a right to resist the enforcement of Federal acts they deemed unconstitutional.

In 1814, at the Hartford Convention, New England leaders talked of secession. . . . A few years afterward, Maryland and Ohio took official action to prevent branches of the Nationally-chartered Bank of the United States from operating within their borders; Ohio went so far as to seize the office and the cash on hand. In Jackson's administration, Georgia defied the Supreme Court and the requirements of a Federal treaty by convicting and hanging a Cherokee Indian under State law. South Carolina threatened nullification over the tariff issue. Among the efforts of northern States to nullify the Fugitive Slave Act of 1850 was the action of the Wisconsin courts in issuing a writ of *habeas corpus* to free a man convicted in a Federal court, after the Supreme Court had specifically denied their authority to do so.

All these challenges from various parts of the country were disposed of peaceably, except for the slavery controversy. Over that issue and secession the North, behind Lincoln's leadership, finally settled by force the ultimate issue of National supremacy. After the war it could no longer be maintained that the Union was only a creature of the States, or a compact among them, liable to be thwarted or dissolved at the will of any of them. From then on, the interpretation of National powers was to be determined, in the main, by some National authority.

WHO FIXES THE BOUNDARIES?

What those powers were, and which National authority was to be the judge of them, were questions not so conclusively settled. Chief Justice Marshall asserted emphatically in 1803 that it was the power and duty of the judiciary to say definitively what the law—including the Constitution—means, when a question is raised in a proper case. But his successor, Chief Justice Taney, found in the doctrine of "political questions" some limits on the judicial power to interpret the supreme law. Further limits are inherent in the nature of the process of judicial review over legislation, confined as it is to cases and controversies. Andrew Jackson and Abraham Lincoln expanded the role of the President in ways the Court could not control, ways that sometimes give that office a decisive voice in determining the scope of National power as well as the direction of National policy. Finally, there are occasions when a congressional enactment is the dominant fact in the settlement of a constitutional controversy, at least for a period of years. This may happen because the congressional action is never subjected to a judicial test; or because the test comes only after the enactment has been in force for a long period of time; or because even when the courts bar one method of achieving an end, Congress finds another way. The Compromise of 1850, the Reconstruction Acts, the Agricultural Adjustment and Fair Labor Standards Acts of 1938, and most recently the legislation leaving the regulation of insurance with the States and the settlement of the Tidelands dispute illustrate such congressional determinations.

From time to time all three branches of the National Government have shown varying attitudes on issues of federalism. On the record of over a century and a half the Supreme Court, except when dealing with slavery, has probably taken the most consistently Nationalist position. While Congress has extended the sphere of National action, it has in many ways responded to locally held sentiments. Mindful of the impact of National action on the institutions of State and local governments, Congress has frequently taken affirmative action to protect their interests. Successive Presidents have taken sharply contrasting positions; some have been forthright advocates of strong National action, while others have been at pains to protect what they thought were the prerogatives of the States.

NATIONAL SUPREMACY UPHELD BY MARSHALL

Supreme Court doctrine on the boundaries of National and State powers illustrates judicial flexibility. Chief Justice Marshall took a strong Federalist line in vindicating National supremacy and in developing the doctrine of implied powers. He marked out a broad area for exclusive National jurisdiction. He sustained congressional authority when it was used, as in chartering the Bank of the United States or in regulating the coastwise trade. Even in the absence of congressional action, he blocked State entry into the National sphere, as by a tax, nondiscriminatory though it might be, on imported goods in their original packages. Marshall also took a stern view of State acts that violated the spirit, if not the letter, of express constitutional restrictions, or that threatened vested property rights. . . .

New administrative undertakings of the [Civil] war and postwar years introduced the National Government permanently into fresh areas of activity. Among these were the first Morrill Act of 1862, which made land grants for agricultural and mechanical colleges in each State; the establishment of a Commissioner (later Secretary) of Agriculture in the same year, and of a Commissioner of Education in 1867; and in 1870 the creation, under the Attorney General, of a Department of Justice to supervise from Washington the activities of the United States attorneys in the field. More important for the business world was the establishment of a National banking system in 1863. This created for the first time a corps of National bank examiners. In a follow-up move, Congress used the taxing power to oust the States from the field of chartering banks of issue. Soon thereafter there was a uniform currency.

THE FOURTEENTH AMENDMENT

The adoption of the Fourteenth Amendment in 1868 overshadowed all these moves in its long-term significance for National-State relations. It announced a national definition of citizenship, something the framers in 1787 had studiously avoided. Many thought the amendment authorized Congress to regulate civil rights generally all over the country, but the Congress soon lost its relish for that assignment. As it turned out, the amendment subjected to the possibility of judicial review in the Federal courts a broad range of State legislation over which the State courts had previously had the final word. By implication, it portended, too, a social revolution in the South. Many years passed, however, before judicial review afforded Negroes much of the protection that was the first and principal object of the amendment. Indeed, for a decade and a half the amendment seemed to have made surprisingly little change. The Supreme Court invalidated the last Civil Rights Act, but was otherwise at pains to stay aloof from most of the constitutional controversies over Reconstruction; and it declined at first to expand the field of its review of State legislation. Indeed, except for the abolition of slavery and of the supposed right of secession, the Reconstruction period ended with the federal balance apparently not far from its position in 1860.

Drastic constitutional changes, nevertheless, were just over the horizon. They had little to do with the issues of the war. They were directed instead to adapting an 18th-century document, written for a decentralized agrarian society, to the political demands of an urban industrial nation.

RESTRICTIONS ON ECONOMIC REGULATION

The details of constitutional interpretation since Reconstruction are too complex for recital here. One persistent trend was the judicial protection of property rights against the growing volume of State legislative and administrative action that attempted to regulate railroads, grain elevators, and other forms of business enterprise. The Supreme Court first recognized corporations as "persons" with standing to invoke the Fourteenth Amendment, and then broadened the meaning of the due process clause of the amendment to give it a substantive, and not merely a procedural, content. What had once been a phrase in the Bill of Rights intended to guarantee the historic forms of trial in criminal cases became by the end of the 19th century a significant constitutional barrier against legislation restricting the liberty of adults to make business contracts. The issue of constitutionality turned on the Court's views as to the reasonableness of the legislation. So a law limiting hours of labor was valid if applied to underground mining, but not to a bakery. Anti-union stipulations in labor contracts could not be outlawed. Price regulations were restricted to public utilities, and subject to a judicial review of their reasonableness.

State regulation was cramped by the commerce clause, too. Illinois was prevented from limiting railroad transportation charges on interstate traffic (1886), and Iowa from stopping the sale of intoxicating liquors coming in from neighboring States (1890), although Congress had not yet expressed a national policy on either subject.

Judicial interpretation of the commerce clause and of the due process clause of the Fifth Amendment also put limits on congressional regulation of business activities. The Sherman Anti-Trust Act of 1890 was constitutional, but for a long time it was held not to apply to manufacturers, on the ground that manufacturing was not commerce; its regulation was, therefore, the province of the States. An attempt to outlaw the "yellow dog" contract in railroad employment was an unconstitutional deprivation of liberty without due process.

To the same general end the Tenth Amendment, reserving to the States or to the people all powers not delegated to the National Government, was sometimes made the basis for a narrow construction of congressional powers. Since child labor and agriculture were not mentioned in the list of enumerated powers, their regulation, it was said, was reserved to the States and could not be reached indirectly by the taxing or commerce powers of Congress.

A corollary doctrine led to the recognition of intergovernmental immunities from taxation, both on the salaries of public officials and on the interest on government bonds.

WHERE REGULATION WAS ALLOWED

While the lines of interpretation just sketched tended to limit both State and National regulation of economic enterprise, other regulations during the late 19th and early 20th centuries were receiving the Court's approval. Public health grounds justified compulsory vaccination of people and sanitary inspection of food. Public safety supported building codes and fire precautions. Humanitarian considerations justified limits on work hours for women in factories. Welfare and social justice sustained workmen's compensation laws altering the common law liabilities of master and servant. The need to protect real estate values supported zoning regulations. Revenue needs validated license taxes on carriers. Thus a considerable area was kept open for the States in spite of the Fourteenth Amendment.

Similarly, the powers of Congress were not always narrowly construed. The Court allowed use of the Federal taxing power to drive out colored oleomargarine and to control narcotics. After 1895 and until the Sixteenth Amendment, an income tax was unconstitutional, but a tax on corporate income was permitted when it was called an excise. During the first two decades of this century, the commerce power was extended to cover railroad holding companies, to enable the Interstate Commerce Commission to bring discriminatory intrastate railroad rates into line, to hamper lotteries, and to attack the white slave traffic. Later, the Court sanctioned the use of this power to pursue kidnapers, stolen property, and fugitives from justice across State lines. To use judicial figures of speech, Congress could "clear interstate commerce of obstructions," could "cleanse it of harmful use," and could control anything in "the stream of commerce." Congress also found a way to divest interstate liquor shipments of their immunity from State law. The treaty power opened the way to the regulation of migratory gamebird hunting. The war power was enough to sustain the first National prohibition law, as well as selective service. The postal power became the basis for fraud orders and bans on obscene publications.

RECENT CHANGES

Two related premises regarding the federal system underlay the judicial interpretation of National and State powers for a full half century after 1880. One was that workably clear and distinct boundaries between their respective realms of activity could be drawn in terms of constitutional powers. The other was that the Supreme Court was the final arbiter of the system. Experience showed both assumptions to be illusory. So many judicial precedents of contrary tendency accumulated that the boundary lines became unpredictable and, indeed, a zone of governmental no man's land sometimes appeared to lie between them. On the major issues of National and State power, the Supreme Court during the early 1900's often had a free choice in decision. Having such a choice, the Court was exposed again, as it had been on some earlier notable occasions, to a crossfire of political criticism. The clash culminated in 1937 when the Court began a series of sweeping reversals or modifications of former decisions.

Since 1937, judicial doctrine has recognized the emergence of a new concept of National-State relations, sometimes labelled "cooperative federalism" in contrast with the separatism of the previous era. The concept rests constitutionally on a broad view of National authority, on the abandonment of the due process clause as a source of substantive restraints on State regulation of economic affairs, and on the Court's refusal to entertain taxpayers' suits challenging exercises of the spending power. Coming full circle after 125 years by the route of implied powers, the Supreme Court now gives to the list of powers delegated to Congress in Article I, Section 8, of the Constitution approximately the same broad sweep of meaning conveyed by the

Virginia Plan. . . . At the same time, the Court has generally refused to invoke the prerogative of review over economic policy that it exercised for 40 years prior to 1937. State and National laws touching economic affairs are no longer held to be deprivations of due process because they conflict with natural rights of property or liberty of contract. The Court has accepted a reading of the general welfare clause that places no discernible judicial limits on the amounts or purposes of Federal spending, although it does not follow that the power to spend carries with it unlimited power to regulate. The potentialities of the spending power were only dimly apprehended before the income tax and the Federal Reserve System opened up new reservoirs of Federal revenues and credit. Grants-in-aid are only one characteristic use of the power, along with many other direct spending and lending programs. Finally, the Court has directed the lower Federal courts to follow State law in handling litigation based on diversity of citizenship, so as to minimize conflicts in the applicable rules of decision.

JUDICIAL REVIEW TODAY

Under judicial doctrine since 1937 the Supreme Court has largely removed itself as a practical factor in determining the economic policies of the States and the Nation. It has not, however, eliminated the historic role of judicial review in our federal system. Two remaining functions are noteworthy here, apart from its task of promoting uniformity of interpretation and filling in the gaps in Federal law. One is the duty of judging when the States have overstepped and encroached on whatever area should be the exclusive domain of Federal regulation, if any, or have actually legislated in conflict with Federal law. The exercise of this function is as old as the Court itself and as recent as the 1955 decision that only the Interstate Commerce Commission, and not a State, can revoke the license of an interstate trucking concern to use the highways.

The other function is very recent in its present-day significance, dating only from 1925, though its roots go back to the Fourteenth

Amendment. This is the guardianship of civil liberties. In the face of its withdrawal from supervision over economic policies, the Court during the past 30 years has become noticeably more stern in construing State responsibilities under the Fourteenth Amendment to protect civil and political rights. Beginning in 1925, earlier doctrine has in effect been reversed, and the guarantees of freedom of speech, press, and religion, as well as some (but not all) of the procedural safeguards in criminal cases written in the Bill of Rights against the National Government, have been read also into the due process clause of the Fourteenth Amendment against the States. More recently, racial discriminations have been brought further under the ban of the equal protection clause of the same amendment. In this whole area, in contrast to the field of economic affairs, the Congress has moved slowly, and the Supreme Court has become the principal instrument of Federal surveillance. There is a surface paradox in this extension of National judicial power at the very time the Court is emphasizing its deference to State legislative policy. But the paradox disappears in a view of the purposes of our federal system which puts the strengthening and preservation of basic personal freedoms among the first objects of the Union.

CONSTITUTIONAL DOCTRINE TODAY

What, then, is the present position of constitutional doctrine as it bears on National-State relations? Reviewing current Supreme Court interpretations in the light of their historical development, the following generalizations appear to be warranted:

First, the constitutional restrictions now applicable to any government in the United States are chiefly procedural, are quite similar in their admonitions to the Nation and to the States, and consequently under the philosophy of these decisions exert no major thrust on the working division of labor and authority between them one way or the other.

These restrictions are found chiefly in the Bill of Rights and the Fourteenth Amendment. They put important limits on the permissible ways of using the coercive powers of government, and on some policies related to the provision of certain services and to the conduct of elections. In the main they have been left to the judiciary to enforce. In the sense that they subject State policies and procedures to a National judicial review, they are a significant feature of our federal system. Court enforcement of them may cut across time-honored policies and deeply felt beliefs. But they do not have the effect of transferring activities from one governmental level to another. Nor do they prevent either level from pursuing substantive programs of any kind likely to be adopted in this country. The federal balance might be different if there were major disparities in the procedural restraints applied at one level in contrast with the other; or if the Congress showed any disposition to make full use of the powers conferred on it by the Fourteenth Amendment.

Second, the prohibitions on the States, express and implied, that keep them from actions deemed to encroach on powers delegated to the National Government have only a minimal effect on the capacity of the States to discharge their functions.

These prohibitions set the lower limits of the zone of National responsibility for governmental action. So far as they have a nationalizing tendency, it comes chiefly from the judiciary in the form of Court review of State action. In general, these limitations keep the States out of interstate commerce, admiralty, bankruptcy, and currency matters, and prevent them from imposing burdens on Federal instrumentalities. It does not follow that these prohibitions on the States automatically or necessarily compel the Congress to act in these fields; this depends on the will of Congress. They do, of course, present some borderline problems that have nevertheless proved manageable. For one thing, the trend of recent judicial opinion outside the civil liberties field has on the whole been tolerant and accommodating to State policy: the States, for instance, can tax some interstate commerce, or set up quarantine inspections at their borders, or fix weight limits for trucks, or enforce highway traffic regulations, provided they do not discriminate against interstate commerce or burden it "unduly." Moreover, congressional waivers or administrative cessions of a National jurisdiction staked out by the Court can make flexible room for State action; this is the pattern made familiar by the Twenty-first (Repeal) Amendment. It is also illustrated in the Tidelands Act, and in the refusal of the National Labor Relations Board to hear some local cases. Even where action by the States is precluded by virtue of positive congressional action, as in some aspects of labor relations, the boundary adjustments are within congressional control. Broadly speaking, the working division of duties is not determined by rigid constitutional limits on the States.

Third, the range of activities that lie primarily within the power of the States by reason of the lack of any coercive authority in Congress to deal with them, is substantial. While the National Government has extensive authority to regulate, especially under its tax and interstate commerce powers, there is still a broad field of regulatory activity beyond its reach. The limits of the delegated and implied National powers fix the maximum range of National action. The existence of such constitutional bounds is probably more important than their exact location for the purpose of maintaining the federal nature of our governmental system. It is important that National powers be adequate to all truly national needs; it is also important that they do not jeopardize the proper functioning of the States. The former object is a matter of power and hence of constitutional law; the latter is primarily a matter of policy. It is improbable that judicial action would be needed to prevent the National military or taxing power, for example, from being used directly on the State governments to destroy or cripple them. The more likely danger is that the National Government will dissipate its energies and prestige, or discourage the States from developing their talents, by taking on matters that lie in the field of concurrent powers and that the States can handle acceptably.

Fourth, the possibility of a significant constitutional no man's land in our federal system has been disposed of by judicial reinterpretations. The early child labor cases, and the decisions invalidating the Municipal Bankruptcy Act and the Bituminous Coal Act during the depression, pointed for a time to subjects beyond the reach of any legislation. But apparently there are no longer any areas of economic policy barred to Congress for want of delegated power, on the one hand, and impractical or unconstitutional for the States to enter, on the other. The States are accorded more latitude now, and National powers are broadly available for all the great exigencies of government for which the Union was created: to "establish Justice, insure domestic Tranquility, provide for the common defence, promote the general Welfare, and secure the Blessings of Liberty * * *"

Fifth, it follows that the basic problems of maintaining our federal system today lie in those areas of National and State power where both Congress and the States have real choices to make, and where many alternative courses of action are open. It is in these areas that practical issues arise and tensions between interested groups and organizations are felt. Legislatures and administrative agencies within their assigned jurisdictions provide the appropriate forums for settling these issues.

Under our federal system, the division of responsibilities between the National Government and the States was once thought to be settled mainly in terms of power: either one level, or both, or neither, had the authority to move; and that was enough to settle their functions. Such a decision was usually one for the judiciary. Under current judicial doctrine, there are still limits on the coercive powers at both levels, but the National powers are broad and the possibilities by means of spending are still broader. The crucial questions now are questions of policy: Which level ought to move? Or should both? Or neither? What are the prudent and proper divisions of labor and responsibility between them? These are questions mainly for legislative judgment, and the criteria are chiefly political, economic, and administrative, rather than legal. The emphasis is on mutual and complementary undertakings in furtherance of common aims. The task of this Commission, accordingly, is to determine, within the constitutional limits of National and State powers, and in the light of 165 years of practical experience, what division of responsibilities is best calculated to sustain a workable basis for intergovernmental relations in the future.

Summary

Our federal system is a unique phenomenon, without an earlier model and bearing only a general resemblance to later federal systems established elsewhere. It is the product partly of human purpose, partly of unconscious adaptation to the circumstances and the felt needs of our people. It has survived the vicissitudes of over a century and a half of our history to become now the oldest federal system. It has met the test of civil war. It has accommodated vast territorial expansion to the significant principle that the new States shall enjoy constitutional equality with the old. It has furnished a governmental environment compatible with unparalleled economic growth and social advances. It has shouldered an increased degree of responsibility for social security and welfare. It has enabled the mustering of resources for waging two world wars and developing atomic energy.

At the same time, it has preserved a degree of local autonomy unmatched among the world's other great powers. The States make their own constitutions, and the laws that govern elections, crimes, property, contracts, torts, domestic relations, and the like. Most States in their turn have tended in practice to establish a virtually federal division of powers and responsibilities between themselves, their counties, and their municipalities. This autonomy has kept under local controls most of the schools, the police, the ordinary administration of criminal and civil justice, the local taxes, and the provision of most municipal services. It has kept in local hands also the machinery of elections and with it, in the main, the control of the party system. It has enabled local option to prevail on a wide range of domestic concerns. It has furnished local bases of power and refuge for political leaders, parties, and policies in opposition to those for the time being dominant in Washington. It has made possible a large degree of popular participation and consent. . . .

STATE VS. FEDERAL POWER:

A SCHOOL INTEGRATION CASE

Appomattox confirmed that the national government is supreme within its sphere of powers; but in a dynamic federal system, that sphere must be constantly redefined. A recurrent controversy has turned on the question: who shall decide whether the residual "sovereignty" of the states has been infringed upon by an allegedly unconstitutional act of an organ of the national government? The authority of the Supreme Court as final arbiter was recently challenged again by the interposition of state power to prevent enforcement of judicial orders against compulsory racial segregation in public school education. In the Little Rock case, in 1957, President Eisenhower removed the "interposers" with the United States Army. In the New Orleans case, in 1960, the United States Court of Appeals, Fifth Circuit, sustaining the ultimate authority of the Supreme Court, ruled unconstitutional the doctrine of state interposition.

CALLED into extraordinary session for November 4, 1960, just ten days before the day fixed by this court for the partial desegregation of the New Orleans public schools, the Louisiana Legislature promptly enacted 25 measures designed to halt, or at least forestall, the implementation of the Orleans Parish School Board's announced proposal to admit five Negro girls of first grade age to formerly all-white schools. The first of these, Act 2 of the First Extraordinary Session of 1960, is the so-called "interposition" statute by which Louisiana declares that it will not recognize the Supreme Court's decision in Brown v. Board of Education, supra, or the orders of this

Bush *v.* Orleans Parish School Board, 188 F. Supp. 916 (Nov. 30, 1960).

court issued pursuant to the mandate of that case. Insofar as it provides criminal penalties against federal judges and United States marshals who render or carry out such decisions, the Government, by separate suit consolidated here for hearing, seeks an injunction against the Act. The next seven Acts, Nos. 3 through 9, merely repeal statutes earlier ruled on by this court and enjoined as unconstitutional.

The remaining seventeen Acts, numbered 10 through 14 and 16 through 27, are here assailed on constitutional grounds and a temporary injunction against their enforcement is prayed for by the plaintiffs, parents of white school children, in the Williams case. Among these are measures purporting to abolish the Orleans Parish School Board and transfer its function to the Legislature. On November 10, 1960, restraining orders were directed to the appropriate state officers enjoining them from enforcing the provisions of all but one of the statutes in suit pending hearing before this court. Nevertheless, apparently still considering itself the administrator of the New Orleans public schools, the Louisiana Legislature has continued to act in that capacity, issuing its directives by means of concurrent resolutions. House Concurrent Resolutions Nos. 17, 18 and 19. On November 13th, when the enforcement of these resolutions was also restrained on motion of the School Board, the Legislature retaliated by addressing all but one member of the Board out of office. House Concurrent Resolution No. 23. This action by the Legislature also was the subject of an immediate temporary restraining order. As cross-claimant in the Bush case, the original school case filed by parents of Negro children, the School Board now asks for a temporary injunction against these most recent measures. Finally, the court has before it a motion by the School Board to vacate or stay its order fixing November 4, 1960, as the date for the partial desegregation of the local schools. . . .

Interposition

Except for an appropriation measure to provide for the cost of the special session, the very first statute enacted by the Louisiana Legislature at this Extraordinary Session was the interposition act. That was appropriate because it is this declaration which sets the tone and gives substance to all the subsequent legislation. For the most part, the measures that followed merely implement the resolve announced in the interposition act to "maintain racially separate public school facilities *** when such facilities are in the best interest of their citizens," notwithstanding "the decisions of the Federal District Courts in the State of Louisiana, prohibiting the maintenance of separate schools for whites and negroes and ordering said schools to be racially integrated," which decisions, being "based solely and entirely on the pronouncements of Brown vs. Topeka Board of Education," are "null, void and of no effect as to the State of Louisiana." Significantly, the Attorney General, appearing for the State and most of its officers, rested his sole defense on this act. Without question, the nub of the controversy is in the declaration of interposition. If it succeeds, there is no occasion to look further, for the state is then free to do as it will in the field of public education. On the other hand, should it fail, nothing can save the "package" of segregation measures to which it is tied.

Interposition is an amorphous concept based on the proposition that the United States is a compact of states, any one of which may interpose its sovereignty against the enforcement within its borders of any decision of the Supreme Court or act of Congress, irrespective of the fact that the constitutionality of the act has been established by decision of the Supreme Court. Once interposed, the law or decision would then have to await approval by constitutional amendment before enforcement within the interposing state. In essence, the doctrine denies the constitutional obligation of the states to respect those decisions of the Supreme Court with which they do not agree.[1] The doctrine may have had some validity under the Articles of Confederation. On their failure, however, "in order to form a more perfect union," the *people*, not the states, of this country ordained and estab-

[1] The short answer to interposition may be found in Cooper v. Aaron, 353 U.S. 1, 17-18. . . .

lished the Constitution. Martin v. Hunter, 14 U.S. (1 Wheat.) 304, 324. Thus the keystone of the interposition thesis, that the United States is a compact of states, was disavowed in the Preamble to the Constitution.[2]

Nevertheless, throughout the early history of this country, the standard of interposition was raised whenever a state strongly disapproved of some action of the central government. Perhaps the most precise formulation of the doctrine can be found in the Virginia and Kentucky interposition resolutions against the Alien and Sedition Acts. Jefferson was the reluctant author of the Kentucky resolution, while Madison wrote Virginia's. Jefferson was not proud of his work for he never admitted authorship. And Madison, after publicly espousing the cause of interposition for a short time, spent much of his energy combatting the doctrine and finally admitted its bankruptcy in these words:

> The jurisdiction claimed for the Federal Judiciary is truly the only defensive armor of the Federal Government, or rather for the Constitution and laws of the United States. Strip it of that armor, and the door is wide open for nullification, anarchy and convulsion, * * *—Letter, April 1, 1833, quoted in 1 Warren, The Supreme Court in United States History (Revised Ed. 1926), 740.

While there have been many cases which treat of segmented facets of the interposition doctrine, in only one is the issue squarely presented. In United States v. Peters, 9 U.S. (5 Cranch) 115, the legislature of Pennsylvania interposed the sovereignty of that state against a decree of the United States District Court sitting in Pennsylvania. After much litigation, Chief Justice Marshall finally laid the doctrine to rest thusly:

> If the legislature of the several states may, at will, annul the judgments of the courts of the United States, and destroy the rights acquired under those judgments, the Constitution itself becomes a solemn mockery; and the nation is deprived of the means of enforcing its laws by the instrumen-

[2] Of course, even the "compact theory" does not justify interposition. Thus, Edward Livingston, Louisiana's noted lawgiver, though an adherent of that theory, strongly denied the right of a state to nullify federal law or the decisions of the federal courts. . . .

tality of its own tribunals. So fatal a result must be deprecated by all; and the people of Pennsylvania, not less than the citizens of every other state, must feel a deep interest in resisting principles so destructive of the Union, and in averting consequences so fatal to themselves.—United States v. Peters, supra, 136.

Interposition theorists concede the validity, under the supremacy clause, of acts of Congress and decisions of the Supreme Court except in the area reserved for the states by the Tenth Amendment. But laws and decisions in this reserved area, the argument runs, are by definition *unconstitutional*, hence are not governed by the supremacy clause and do not rightly command obedience. This, of course, is Louisiana's position with reference to the Brown decision in the recent Act of Interposition. Quite obviously, as an inferior court, we cannot overrule that decision. The issue before us is whether the Legislature[3] of Louisiana may do so.

Assuming always that the claim of interposition is an appeal to legality, the inquiry is who, under the Constitution, has the final say on questions of constitutionality, who delimits the Tenth Amendment. In theory, the issue might have been resolved in several ways. But, as a practical matter, under our federal system the only solution short of anarchy was to assign the function to *one supreme court*. That the final decision should rest with the judiciary rather than the legislature was inherent in the concept of constitutional government in which legislative acts are subordinate to the paramount organic law, and, if only to avoid "a hydra in government from which nothing but contradiction and confusion can proceed," final authority had to be centralized in a single national court. *The Federalist*, Nos. 78, 80, 81, 82. As Madison said before the adoption of the Constitution: "Some such tribunal is clearly essential to prevent an appeal to the sword and a dissolution of the compact; and that it ought to be

[3] It is interesting to note that even Calhoun, whose writings, in addition to those of Madison, are now invoked by Louisiana, did not pretend that the *legislature* of the state had a right to interpose, but held that a popular *convention* within the state was the proper medium for asserting state sovereignty. See his "Fort Hill Letter" of August 28, 1832, quoted in pertinent part in Miller and Howell, "Interposition, Nullification and the Delicate Division of Power in a Federal System," 5 J. Pub. L.2, 31.

established under the general rather than under the local governments, or, to speak more properly, that it could be safely established
under the first alone, is a position not likely to be combatted." *The
Federalist*, No. 39.

And so, from the beginning, it was decided that the Supreme Court
of the United States must be the final arbiter on questions of constitutionality. It is, of course, the guardian of the Constitution against
encroachments by the national Congress. Marbury v. Madison, supra.
But more important to our discussion is the constitutional role of the
Court with regard to State acts. The original Judiciary Act of 1789
confirmed the authority of the Supreme Court to review the judgments of all state tribunals on constitutional questions. Acts of Sept.
24, 1789, § 25; 1 Stat. 73, 85, See Martin v. Hunter, supra; Wor-
cester v. Georgia, 31 U.S. (6 Peters) 515; Cohens v. Virginia, 19
U.S. (6 Wheat.) 264; Ableman v. Booth, 62 U.S. (21 Row.) 506.
Likewise from the first one of its functions was to pass on the constitutionality of state laws. Fletcher v. Peck, 10 U.S. (6 Cranch) 87;
McCulloch v. Maryland, 17 U.S. (4 Wheat.) 316. And the duty of
the Court with regard to the acts of the state executive is no different.
Sterling v. Constantin, 287 U.S. 378; Cooper v. Aaron, 358 U.S. 1.
The fact is that the Constitution itself established the Supreme Court
of the United States as the final tribunal for constitutional adjudication. By definition, there can be no appeal from its decisions.

The initial conclusion is obvious enough. Plainly, the states, whose
proceedings are subject to revision by the Supreme Court, can no
more pretend to review that Court's decision on constitutional questions than an inferior can dispute the ruling of an appellate court.
From this alone "it follows that the interpretation of the Fourteenth
Amendment enunciated by [the Supreme] Court in the Brown case
is the supreme law of the land, and [that] Art. VI of the Constitution
makes it of binding effect on the States 'any Thing in the Constitution
or Laws of any State to the Contrary notwithstanding.' " Cooper v.
Aaron, supra, 18.

But this is not all. From the fact that the Supreme Court of the
United States rather than any state authority is the ultimate judge of

constitutionality, another consequence of equal importance results. It is that the jurisdiction of the *lower* federal courts and the correctness of their decisions on constitutional questions cannot be reviewed by the state governments. Indeed, since the appeal from their rulings lies to the Supreme Court of the United States, as the only authoritative Constitutional tribunal, neither the executive, nor the legislature, nor even the courts of the state, have any competence in the matter. It necessarily follows that, pending review by the Supreme Court, the decisions of the subordinate federal courts on constitutional questions have the authority of the supreme law of the land and must be obeyed. Assuredly, this is a great power, but a necessary one. See United States v. Peters, supra, 135, 136.

Apprehensive of the validity of the proposition that the Constitution is a compact of states, interposition asserts that at least a ruling challenged by a state should be suspended until the people can ratify it by constitutional amendment. But this invocation of "constitutional processes" is a patent subterfuge. Unlike open nullification, it is defiance hiding under the cloak of apparent legitimacy. The obvious flaw in the argument lies in the unfounded insistence that *pending a vote on the proposed amendment* the questioned decision must be voided. Even assuming their good faith in proposing an amendment against themselves, the interpositionists want too much. Without any semblance of legality, they claim the right at least temporarily to annul the judgment of the highest court, and, should they succeed in defeating the amendment proposed, they presume to interpret that victory as voiding forever the challenged decision. It requires no elaborate demonstration to show that this is a preposterous perversion of Article V of the Constitution. Certainly the Constitution can be amended "to overrule" the Supreme Court. But there is nothing in Article V that justifies the presumption that what has authoritatively been declared to be the law ceases to be the law while the amendment is pending, or that the non-ratification of an amendment alters the Constitution or any decisions rendered under it.[4]

---

[4] Madison also had occasion to comment on this modified interposition: "* * * We have seen the absurdity of such a claim in its naked and suicidal form. Let us turn to it as modi-

The conclusion is clear that interposition is not a *constitutional* doctrine. If taken seriously, it is illegal defiance of constitutional authority. Otherwise, "it amounts to no more than a protest, an escape valve through which the legislatures blow off steam to relieve their tensions." Shuttleworth v. Birmingham Board of Education, N.D. Ala., 162 F Supp. 372, 381. However solemn or spirited, interposition resolutions have no legal efficiency. Such, in substance, is the official view of Virginia, delivered by its present Governor while Attorney General. And there is a general tacit agreement among the other interposing states which is amply reflected in their failure even to raise the argument in the recent litigation, the outcome of which they so much deplore. Indeed, Louisiana herself has had an "interposition" resolution on the books since 1956, and has never brought it forth. The enactment of the resolution in statutory form does not change its substance. Act 2 of the First Extraordinary Session of 1960 is not legislation in the true sense. It neither requires nor denies. It is mere statement of principles, a political polemic, which provides the predicate for the second segregation packages of 1960, the legislation in suit. Its unconstitutional premise strikes with nullity all that it would support.

---

fied by South Carolina, into a right of every State to resist within itself the execution of a Federal law deemed by it to be unconstitutional, and to demand a convention of the States to decide the question of constitutionality; the annulment of the law to continue in the meantime, and to be permanent unless three-fourths of the States concur in overruling the annulment.

"Thus, during the temporary nullification of the law, the results would be the same from (as?) those proceeding from an unqualified nullification, and the result of the convention might be that seven out of twenty-four States might make the temporary results permanent. It follows, that any State which could obtain the concurrence of six others might abrogate any law of the United States, constructively, whatever, and give to the Constitution any shape they please, in opposition to the construction and will of the other seventeen, each of the seventeen have an equal right and authority with each of the seven. Every feature in the Constitution might thus be successively changed; and after a scene of unexampled confusion and distraction, what had been unanimously agreed to as a whole, would not, as a whole, be agreed to by a single party. The amount of this modified right of nullification is, that a single State may arrest the operation of a law of the United States, and institute a process which is to terminate in the ascendancy of a minority over a large majority in a republican system, the characteristic rule of which is, that the major will is the ruling will. * * *" Madison, On Nullification (1835-1836), in IV Letters and Other Writings of James Madison, Congress ed. (1865), 409.

COOPERATIVE FEDERALISM

Although conflicts between the states and the national government are sometimes sensational, cooperation is the continuing characteristic of the federal system. The partnership between the two levels of government is embodied in the grant-in-aid programs which are utilized to achieve a variety of national objectives by congressional legislation on subjects traditionally within state jurisdiction, such as school lunches, maternity care, forest-fire prevention, cancer control, highway construction, and slum clearance. The national government creates the program, establishes the standards, and furnishes much of the money (about 15% of total state revenues), often on a matching basis, while the states or cities administer the program. Thus, the grant-in-aid device considerably extends the scope of national powers, yet strengthens the federal system and the vitality of the states. Here is a description of the "public assistance" grant program which was established by the Social Security Act of 1935 and which benefited almost six million people in 1960.

Purpose of the Program

*T*HE PURPOSE of grants-in-aid for public assistance is to help the States promote and achieve a measure of economic security for their citizens. The grants-in-aid are designed specifically to provide help to the States to give aid to the needy aged, the blind, children who have been deprived of parental care and support, and to the disabled.

The Commission on Intergovernmental Relations, *A Description of Twenty-five Federal Grant-in-Aid Programs* (Washington: G.P.O., 1955), pp. 112-117.

(The act also makes provision for grants to States to enable them to extend and strengthen maternal and child health services, services for crippled children and other child welfare services, and also a system of old-age and survivors' insurance which is administered entirely by the Federal Government.) The term "public assistance" as used in the act comprehends the aid given to needy persons in the following four categories: Title I, Old-age assistance; title IV, Aid to dependent children; title X, Aid to the blind; title XIV, Aid to the permanently and totally disabled. As it has evolved and actually operated, the program has remained generally in accordance with its original purpose.

Nature of the Program

It is a joint enterprise of the Federal and State Governments in which the Federal Government contributes money to the States on a matching basis, providing the States meet certain conditions. The four categories of assistance may be described in general terms as follows: Funds for old-age assistance are provided for needy persons over 65 years of age. Dependent children are those under 16 years of age (18 if regularly attending school) who are living with a parent or near relative and who have been deprived of parental support or care by reason of the death, continued absence from the home, or physical or mental incapacity of a parent. The "blind" include needy persons having insufficient vision to perform tasks for which sight is essential, as well as persons without any vision. The permanently and totally disabled are needy individuals who suffer from physical disabilities which render them incapable of any useful employment.

State Plan and Budget

The Social Security Act requires that each State, in order to qualify for Federal aid for public assistance in any one of these categories, must have a plan which, in effect, describes a program for administering public assistance within the State. This plan becomes the working basis for administering the function within the State. The plan is required by the Social Security Act to include, in all of the categorical programs, the following:

1. Effectiveness of the plan in all political subdivisions.
2. Financial participation by the State.
3. Administration or supervision of administration of the plan by a single State agency.
4. Opportunity for a fair hearing to any individual whose claim for assistance is denied or not acted upon with reasonable promptness.
5. Methods of administration which will produce proper and efficient operation of the plan (this includes the establishment and maintenance of personnel standards on a merit basis).
6. Reports by the State agency, in such form, and containing such information as the Federal Government may from time to time require, and compliance with such provisions as the Federal Government may find necessary to assure the correctness and verification of such reports.
7. Taking into consideration any other income and resources available to the recipient (with a specific exception in the case of aid to the blind).
8. Safeguards which restrict the use or disclosure of information concerning the applicants and recipients to purposes directly connected with the administration of assistance.
9. Opportunity to apply to all who wish to do so; and the furnishing of assistance with reasonable promptness to all persons eligible.

For old-age assistance, aid to the blind, and aid to the disabled, if the plan includes payments to individuals in private or public institutions, the plan must provide for the establishment or designation of a State authority or authorities which shall be responsible for establishing and maintaining standards for such institutions. For aid to dependent children the plan must provide for prompt notice to appropriate law enforcement officials of the fact that aid is being given in respect of a child who has been deserted or abandoned by a parent.

The plans for aid to dependent children, aid to the blind, and aid to the disabled must include provisions which prevent an individual from receiving more than one of the four types of assistance at the same time. As to the blind, it is provided that consideration of other sources of support—earnings up to the amount of $50 per month—shall *not* be considered. For the blind, the aged, and the totally disabled, the law provides that any plan to be approved shall not make any residence restriction which bars a person who has resided in the State for 5 years during the 9 years immediately preceding the application for aid. For dependent children, the plan may not impose a residence requirement denying aid to a child who has resided in the State for one year immediately preceding the application, or if the parent or other relative has resided in the State one year immediately preceding the birth of the child. For the totally disabled, the blind, and the aged, the plan may not exclude any person who is a United States citizen from making application.

Each State plan is subject to the approval of the Secretary of the Department of Health, Education, and Welfare.

Federal Field Personnel Required

Public assistance field representatives are stationed in each of the regional offices maintained by the Department of Health, Education, and Welfare. Each of the regional offices is organized with a regional director and the following officers: Regional attorney, regional merit system representative, regional auditor, regional surplus utilization representative, a representative of the Public Health Service, various representatives of the Social Security Administration, a representative of Vocational Rehabilitation, and representatives of the Office of Education.

Reports and Audits

Each State is required to make periodic reports in such form as the Department of Health, Education, and Welfare may from time to time request. Such reports include information on fiscal and operating methods in each of the States and on inspections of agency records and procedures. Each State is required to maintain accounts and all of the necessary supporting documents so as to permit, at any time, accurate and expeditious determination of the status of Federal grants including the disposition of all monies received and the nature and amount of all charges claimed to lie against the respective Federal authorizations. Inasmuch as there are four separate categories of public assistance, even though the formulas for three of them are identical and for the fourth one similar in principle, the calculations for the amounts of money in Federal aid must be computed separately for each category. This makes the accounting systems somewhat complex and a considerable amount of paper work is required.

Withholding of Payment

Whenever it appears that there is a failure on the part of any State to comply substantially with any provision of the Social Security Act, or of the provisions of the approved plan of the State for administration of the function, the Secretary of the Department of Health, Education, and Welfare, after affording the State an opporunity for a hearing, may, within his discretion, refuse to certify further payments to the State until he is satisfied that satisfactory measures have been taken to correct the condition. The power of the Secretary of Health, Education, and Welfare to withhold payment has been exercised in rare instances, and seldom has threatened action been taken to withhold payment. Such action obviously would be a source of irritation to the States.

Federal Administrative Supervision

Supervision of State operations is maintained through the regional offices. It is expected that an inspection of State administrative operations will be made at least once each year. Where it appears that special attention is needed to any unusual situation arising in the State, more extended time may be given to such a situation by the regional office consultants. All reports of State operations are reviewed with care by a staff maintained at Washington for that purpose. The supervision exercised may often have a direct effect upon the policies and practices of State and local administrations. In many instances the inspections result in lengthy reports and entail voluminous correspondence. A great deal of routine paperwork is involved as the Washington office and the respective regional offices are kept informed of most details of Federal-State relations. Close contacts with the States are maintained through these regional offices. The inspections pertain very largely to the keeping of records and the adequacy and efficiency of the casework done by the field workers throughout the State. Routine inspections often include spot checking the casework files in various city and county agencies. Reports of such inspections are made to the central office in Washington, D.C., through the regional directors.

Control Over State Personnel

Each State, in order to qualify for grants-in-aid, is required to establish and maintain a merit system (of personnel administration) for employees in the administration of any of the categories in public assistance. The language of the act (title 1, Section 2 (a) 5, title IV, section 402 (a) 5, and title X, section 1002 (a) 5) reads:

"A State plan for old-age assistance must * * * provide such methods of administration (including after January 1, 1940, methods relating to the establishment and maintenance of personnel standards on a merit basis, except that the Administrator shall exercise no authority with respect to the selection, tenure of office, and compensation of any individual employed in accordance with such methods) as are found by the Administrator to be necessary for the proper and efficient operation of the plan * * *"

The Social Security Administration has established specific standards for the operation of a merit system in the States. . . . These standards cover such subjects of public personnel administration as an independent agency to administer the system, a classification and a compensation plan, recruitment, and appointment of personnel, promotions, service ratings, and restrictions on political activity. All existing personnel in State and local agencies at the time the act took effect were required to qualify in open competitive examinations in order to hold their jobs. These requirements for public personnel administration also affect State services where grants-in-aid in public health are made.

A Division of State Merit Systems is maintained in the Office of Field Services of the Department of Health, Education, and Welfare in Washington, and representatives of this division are located in each of the regional offices. Regular inspections of the operation of the personnel systems in the States are made and personnel technicians are available for consultation services on request.

Fiscal Characteristics

Allotment Criteria and Matching Requirements.—Under the categorical programs for the aged (old-age assistance), the blind (aid to the blind), and the disabled (aid to the permanently and totally disabled), the States are eligible to receive Federal grants for each recipient amounting to $20 of the first $25 paid monthly by the State, plus one-half of the remainder of the State's payment up to a maximum Federal grant of $35. Under approved State programs of aid to dependent children, the Federal Government will match State and local payments at the rate of $12 of the first $15 for each child, and one-half of the remainder up to a monthly total Federal grant of $19.50 for the first child and $15 for each succeeding child in a family. In addition, the Federal Government pays one-half of certain administrative expenses incurred by the States in all of the above categories.

Federal and State Contributions.—Total fiscal year 1953 expenditures by the Federal Government for public assistance grants-in-aid total approximately $1.3 billion [over $2 billion in 1960]. . . . Fiscal year 1953 expenditures for old-age assistance totaled $1.6 billion from all sources—55 percent Federal, 39 percent State, and 6 percent local.

The old-age assistance program accounts for the bulk of public assistance expenditures—approximately two-thirds of the total. One-quarter of 1953 funds were spent on aid to dependent children and the remainder (about 8 percent) was divided between aid to the blind and aid to the permanently and totally disabled.

Administrative Expenses (Federal).—For fiscal year 1953, administrative expenses of this program totaled $1,638,000, or 0.1 percent of the total Federal grant expenditure of $1,329,933,470 for that year.

Coverage of Program.—All States, the 2 Territories, and Puerto Rico and the Virgin Islands participated in the old-age assistance and aid to the blind programs; all except Nevada received Federal aid for dependent children; and there were 39 federally approved programs in operation for aid to the permanently and totally disabled.

II. How Representative?

THE NATIONAL PARTY SYSTEM

For reasons of history, custom, and practicality, the United States has a two-party system—at least during Presidential campaigns. The quadrennial national federations of state and local parties, in an effort to win the Presidency by obtaining the constitutionally required majority vote of the electoral college, eschew ideology in the European sense, seek to become all things to all men, and appeal to substantially similar regional, interest-group, and class support. Should a minor or "third" party appear with an attractive program, one of the major parties invariably steals its thunder to retain votes. Third parties, which are narrowly programmatic or extremist, find little support because in the United States there are no large classes of disadvantaged or impoverished people, nor of declassed or alienated people. Freedom, the economy of abundance, and an open-class society have given the overwhelming majority of the people a sense of hope and a stake in the ongoing system. Political opinion operates substantially within a realm of consensus, despite sharp internal differences. The major parties, which reflect that consensus, are the oldest operating political parties in the world—and may be showing signs of hardening of the arteries. In the following selection, from the report of a very distinguished committee of professional political scientists, the major parties are sharply criticized for their incapacity or unwillingness to carry out their programs. The suggested reforms are as timely today as when originally made.

71

The Role of the Political Parties

1. *The Parties and Public Policy*. Throughout this report political parties are treated as indispensable instruments of government. That is to say, we proceed on the proposition that *popular government . . . requires political parties which provide the electorate with a proper range of choice between alternatives of action.* The party system thus serves as the main device for bringing into continuing relationship those ideas about liberty, majority rule and leadership which Americans are largely taking for granted.

For the great majority of Americans, the most valuable opportunity to influence the course of public affairs is the choice they are able to make between the parties in the principal elections. While in an election the party alternative necessarily takes the form of a choice between candidates, putting a particular candidate into office is not an end in itself. The concern of the parties with candidates, elections and appointments is misunderstood if it is assumed that parties can afford to bring forth aspirants for office without regard to the views of those so selected. Actually, the party struggle is concerned with the direction of public affairs. Party nominations are no more than a means to this end. In short, party politics inevitably involves public policy in one way or another. *In order to keep the parties apart, one must consider the relations between each and public policy.*

This is not to ignore that in the past the American two-party system has shown little propensity for evolving original or creative ideas about public policy; that it has even been rather sluggish in responding to such ideas in the public interest; that it reflects in an enlarged way those differences throughout the country which are expressed in the operation of the federal structure of government; and that in all political organizations a considerable measure of irrationality manifests itself.

Giving due weight to each of these factors, we are nevertheless led

The Committee on Political Parties (E. E. Schattschneider, Chairman) of the American Political Science Association, *Toward a More Responsible Two-Party System. The American Political Science Review*, No. 3, Part 2, Supplement (Sept. 1950), pp. 15-36.

to conclude that the choices provided by the two-party system are valuable to the American people in proportion to their definition in terms of public policy. *The reasons for the growing emphasis on public policy in party politics are to be found, above all, in the very operations of modern government.* With the extraordinary growth of the responsibilities of government, the discussion of public affairs for the most part makes sense only in terms of public policy.

2. *The New Importance of Program.* One of the most pressing requirements of contemporary politics is for the party in power to furnish a general kind of direction over the government as a whole. *The crux of public affairs lies in the necessity for more effective formulation of general policies and programs and for better integration of all of the far-flung activities of modern government.*

Only large-scale and representative political organizations possess the qualifications needed for these tasks. The ascendancy of national issues in an industrial society, the impact of the widening concern of government with problems of the general welfare, the entrance into the realm of politics of millions of new voters—all of these factors have tended to broaden the base of the parties as the largest political organizations in the country. *It is in terms of party programs that political leaders can attempt to consolidate public attitudes toward the work plans of government.*

Modern public policy, therefore, accentuates the importance of the parties, not as mere brokers between different groups and interests, but as agencies of the electorate. Because it affects unprecedented numbers of people and because it depends for its execution on extensive and widespread public support, modern public policy requires a broad political base. That base can be provided only by the parties, which reach people touched by no other political organization.

3. *The Potentialities of the Party System. The potentialities of the two-party system are suggested, on the one hand, by the fact that for all practical purposes the major parties monopolize elections; and, on the other, by the fact that both parties have in the past managed to adapt themselves to the demands made upon them by external necessities.*

Moreover, in contrast with any other political organization today in existence, the major parties even now are forced to consider public policy at least broadly enough to make it likely for them to win elections. If public esteem of the parties is much less high than it might be, the depressed state of their reputation has resulted in the main from their past indifference to broadly conceived public policy. This indifference has fixed in the popular mind the idea of spoils, patronage and plunder. It is hence not astonishing when one hears a chosen representative assert for the public ear that in his state "people put principles above party." Much of the agitation for nonpartisanship— despite the impossibility of nonpartisan organization on a national level—is rooted in the same attitudes.

Bad reputations die hard, but things are no longer what they used to be. Certainly success in presidential campaigns today is based on broad national appeals to the widest possible constituencies. To a much greater extent than in the past, elections are won by influences and trends that are felt throughout the country. *It is* therefore *good practical politics to reconsider party organization in the light of the changing conditions of politics. . . .*

What Kind of Party System Is Needed?

There is little point to talking about the American party system in terms of its deficiencies and potentialities except against a picture of what the parties ought to be. Our report would be lacking in exactness without an indication of the sort of model we have in mind.

Americans are reasonably well agreed about the purposes served by the two major parties as long as the matter is discussed in generalities. When specific questions are raised, however, agreement is much more limited. We cannot assume, therefore, a commonly shared view about the essential characteristics of the party system. But we can and must state our own view.

In brief, our view is this: *The party system that is needed must be democratic, responsible and effective*—a system that is accountable to

①

the public, respects and expresses differences of opinion, and is able to cope with the great problems of modern government. Some of the implications warrant special statement, which is the purpose of this section.

A STRONGER TWO-PARTY SYSTEM

1. *The Need for an Effective Party System.* In an era beset with problems of unprecedented magnitude at home and abroad, it is dangerous to drift without a party system that helps the nation to set a general course of policy for the government as a whole. In a two-party system, when both parties are weakened or confused by internal divisions or ineffective organization it is the nation that suffers. When the parties are unable to reach and pursue responsible decisions, difficulties accumulate and cynicism about all democratic institutions grows.

An effective party system requires, first, that the parties are able to bring forth programs to which they commit themselves and, second, that the parties possess sufficient internal cohesion to carry out these programs. In such a system, the party program becomes the work program of the party, so recognized by the party leaders in and out of the government, by the party body as a whole, and by the public. This condition is unattainable unless party institutions have been created through which agreement can be reached about the general position of the party.

Clearly *such a degree of unity within the parties cannot be brought about without party procedures that give a large body of people an opportunity to share in the development of the party program.* One great function of the party system is to bring about the widest possible consent in relation to defined political goals, which provides the majority party with the essential means of building public support for the policies of the government. Democratic procedures in the internal affairs of the parties are best suited to the development of agreement within each party.

2. *The Need for an Effective Opposition Party.* The argument

for a stronger party system cannot be divorced from measures designed to make the parties more fully accountable to the public. *The fundamental requirement of such accountability is a two-party system in which the opposition party acts as the critic of the party in power, developing, defining and presenting the policy alternatives which are necessary for a true choice in reaching public decisions.*

Beyond that, the case for the American two-party system need not be restated here. The two-party system is so strongly rooted in the political traditions of this country and public preference for it is so well established that consideration of other possibilities seems entirely academic. When we speak of the parties without further qualification, we mean throughout our report the two major parties. The inference is not that we consider third or minor parties undesirable or ineffectual within their limited orbit. Rather, we feel that the minor parties in the longer run have failed to leave a lasting imprint upon both the two-party system and the basic processes of American government.

In spite of the fact that the two-party system is part of the American political tradition, it cannot be said that the role of the opposition party is well understood. This is unfortunate because democratic government is greatly influenced by the character of the opposition party. The measures proposed elsewhere in our report to help the party in power to clarify its policies are equally applicable to the opposition.

The opposition most conducive to responsible government is an organized party opposition, produced by the organic operation of the two-party system. When there are two parties identifiable by the kinds of action they propose, the voters have an actual choice. On the other hand, the sort of opposition presented by a coalition that cuts across party lines, as a regular thing, tends to deprive the public of a meaningful alternative. When such coalitions are formed after the elections are over, the public usually finds it difficult to understand the new situation and to reconcile it with the purpose of the ballot. Moreover, on that basis it is next to impossible to hold either party responsible for its political record. This is a serious source of public discontent.

BETTER INTEGRATED PARTIES

1. *The Need for a Party System with Greater Resistance to Pressure.* As a consciously defined and consistently followed line of action keeps individuals from losing themselves in irresponsible ventures, so a program-conscious party develops greater resistance against the inroads of pressure groups.

The value of special-interest groups in a diversified society made up of countless groupings and specializations should be obvious. But organized interest groups cannot do the job of the parties. Indeed, it is only when a working formula of the public interest in its *general* character is made manifest by the parties in terms of coherent programs that the claims of interest groups can be adjusted on the basis of political responsibility. Such adjustment, once again, calls for the party's ability to honor its word.

There is little to suggest that the phenomenal growth of interest organizations in recent decades has come to its end. Organization along such lines is a characteristic feature of our civilization. To some extent these interest groups have replaced or absorbed into themselves older local institutions in that they make it possible for the government and substantial segments of the nation to maintain contact with each other. It must be obvious, however, that *the whole development makes necessary a reinforced party system that can cope with the multiplied organized pressures*. The alternative would be a scheme perhaps best described as government by pressure groups intent upon using the parties to deflect political attention from themselves.

By themselves, the interest groups cannot attempt to define public policy democratically. Coherent public policies do not emerge as the mathematical result of the claims of all of the pressure groups. The integration of the interest groups into the political system is a function of the parties. Any tendency in the direction of a strengthened party system encourages the interest groups to align themselves with one or the other of the major parties. Such a tendency is already at work. One of the noteworthy features of contemporary American politics is the fact that not a few interest groups have found it impossible to remain neutral toward both parties. To illustrate, the entry of organized labor upon the political scene has in turn impelled antagonistic special interests to coalesce in closer political alignments.

In one respect the growth of the modern interest groups is exerting a direct effect upon the internal distribution of power within the parties. They counteract and offset local interests; they are a nationalizing influence. Indeed, the proliferation of interest groups has been one of the factors in the rise of national issues because these groups tend to organize and define their objectives on a national scale.

Parties whose political commitments count are of particular significance to interest organizations with large membership such as exist among industrial workers and farmers, but to a lesser extent also among businessmen. Unlike the great majority of pressure groups, these organizations through their membership—and in proportion to their voting strength—are able to play a measurable role in elections. Interest groups of this kind are the equivalent of organizations of voters. For reasons of mutual interest, the relationship between them and the parties tends to become explicit and continuing.

A stronger party system is less likely to give cause for the deterioration and confusion of purposes which sometimes passes for compromise but is really an unjustifiable surrender to narrow interests. *Compromise among interests is compatible with the aims of a free society only when the terms of reference reflect an openly acknowledged concept of the public interest.* There is every reason to insist that the parties be held accountable to the public for the compromises they accept.

2. *The Need for a Party System with Sufficient Party Loyalty.* It is here not suggested, of course, that the parties should disagree about everything. Parties do not, and need not, take a position on all questions that allow for controversy. The proper function of the parties is to develop and define policy alternatives on matters likely to be of interest to the whole country, on issues related to the responsibility of the parties for the conduct of either the government or the opposition.

Needed clarification of party policy in itself *will not cause the parties to differ more fundamentally or more sharply than they have in the past.* The contrary is much more likely to be the case. The clarification of party policy may be expected to produce a more reasonable discussion of public affairs, more closely related to the political performance of the parties in their actions rather than their words. *Nor is it to be assumed that increasing concern with their programs will cause the parties to erect between themselves an ideological wall.* There is no real ideological division in the American electorate, and hence programs of action presented by responsible parties for the voter's support could hardly be expected to reflect or strive toward such division.

It is true at the same time that ultimately any political party must establish some conditions for membership and place some obligations on its representatives in government. Without so defining its identity the party is in danger of ceasing to be a party. To make party policy effective the *parties have the right and the duty to announce the terms to govern participation in the common enterprise.* This basic proposition is rarely denied, nor are precedents lacking. But there are practical difficulties in the way of applying restraints upon those who disregard the stated terms.

It is obvious that an effective party cannot be based merely or primarily on the expulsion of the disloyal. To impose discipline in any voluntary association is possible only as a last resort and only when a wide consensus is present within the association. Discipline and consensus are simply the front and rear sides of the same coin. *The emphasis in all consideration of party discipline must be,* therefore, *on positive measures to create a strong and general agreement on policies.* Thereafter, the problem of discipline is secondary and marginal.

When the membership of the party has become well aware of party policy and stands behind it, assumptions about teamwork within the party are likely to pervade the whole organization. Ultimately it is the electorate itself which will determine how firmly it wants the lines of party allegiance to be drawn. Yet even a small shift of emphasis toward party cohesion is likely to produce changes not only in the structure of the parties but also in the degree to which members identify themselves with their party.

Party unity is always a relative matter. It may be fostered, but the whole weight of tradition in American politics is against very rigid party discipline. As a general rule, the parties have a basis for expecting adherence to the party program when their position is reasonably explicit. Thus it is evident that the disciplinary difficulties of the parties do not result primarily from a reluctance to impose restraints but from the neglect of positive measures to give meaning to party programs.

As for party cohesion in Congress, the parties have done little to build up the kind of unity within the congressional party that is now so widely desired. Traditionally congressional candidates are treated as if they were the orphans of the political system, with no truly adequate party mechanism available for the conduct of their campaigns. Enjoying remarkably little national or local party support, congressional candidates have mostly been left to cope with the political hazards of their occupation on their own account. *A basis for party cohesion in Congress will be established as soon as the parties interest themselves sufficiently in their congressional candidates to set up strong and active campaign organizations in the constituencies.* Discipline is less a matter of what the parties do *to* their congressional candidates than what the parties do *for* them.

MORE RESPONSIBLE PARTIES

1. *The Need for Parties Responsible to the Public. Party responsibility means the responsibility of both parties to the general public, as enforced in elections.*

Responsibility of the party in power centers on the conduct of the government, usually in terms of policies. The party in power has a responsibility, broadly defined, for the general management of the government, for its manner of getting results, for the results achieved, for the consequences of inaction as well as action, for the intended and unintended outcome of its conduct of public affairs, for all that it plans to do, for all that it might have foreseen, for the leadership it provides, for the acts of all of its agents, and for what it says as well as for what it does.

Party responsibility includes the responsibility of the opposition party, also broadly defined, for the conduct of its opposition, for the management of public discussion, for the development of alternative policies and programs, for the bipartisan policies which it supports, for its failures and successes in developing the issues of public policy, and for its leadership of public opinion. The opposition is as responsible for its record in Congress as is the party in power. It is important that the opposition party be effective but it is equally important that it be responsible, for an irresponsible opposition is dangerous to the whole political system.

Party responsibility to the public, enforced in elections, implies that there be more than one party, for the public can hold a party responsible only if it has a choice. Again, unless the parties identify themselves with programs, the public is unable to make an intelligent choice between them. The public can understand the general management of the government only in terms of policies. When the parties lack the capacity to define their actions in terms of policies, they turn irresponsible because the electoral choice between the parties becomes devoid of meaning.

As a means of achieving responsibility, the clarification of party policy also tends to keep public debate on a more realistic level, restraining the inclination of party spokesmen to make unsubstantiated statements and charges. When party policy is made clear, the result to be expected is a more reasonable and profitable discussion, tied more closely to the record of party action. When there is no clear basis for rating party performance, when party policies cannot be defined in terms of a concrete program, party debate tears itself loose from the facts. Then wild fictions are used to excite the imagination of the public.

2. *The Need for Parties Responsible to Their Members. Party responsibility includes also the responsibility of party leaders to the party membership, as enforced in primaries, caucuses and conventions.*

To this end the internal processes of the parties must be democratic, the party members must have an opportunity to participate in intraparty business, and the leaders must be accountable to the party. Responsibility demands that the parties concern themselves with the development of good relations between the leaders and the members. Only thus can the parties act as intermediaries between the government and the people. Strengthening the parties involves, therefore, the improvement of the internal democratic processes by which the leaders of the party are kept in contact with the members.

The external and the internal kinds of party responsibility need not conflict. Responsibility of party leaders to party members promotes the clarification of party policy when it means that the leaders find it necessary to explain the policy to the membership. Certainly the lack of unity within the membership cannot be overcome by the fiat of an irresponsible party leadership. A democratic internal procedure can be used not merely to test the strength of the various factions within a party but also to resolve the conflicts. The motives for enlarging the areas of agreement within the parties are persuasive because unity is the condition of success.

Intraparty conflict will be minimized if it is generally recognized that national, state and local party leaders have a common responsibility to the party membership. Intraparty conflict is invited and exaggerated by dogmas that assign to local party leaders an exclusive right to appeal to the party membership in their area.

Occasions may arise in which the parties will find it necessary to apply sanctions against a state or local party organization, especially when that organization is in open rebellion against policies established for the whole party. There are a variety of ways in which recognition may be withdrawn. It is possible to refuse to seat delegates to the National Convention; to drop from the National Committee members representing the dissident state organization; to deny legislative committee assignments to members of Congress sponsored by the disloyal organization; and to appeal directly to the party membership in the state or locality, perhaps even promoting a rival organization. The power to take strong measures is there.

It would be unfortunate, however, if the problem of party unity were thought of as primarily a matter of punishment. Nothing prevents the parties from explaining themselves to their own members. The party members have power to insist that local and state party organizations and leaders cooperate with the party as a whole; all the members need is a better opportunity to find out what party politics is about. The need for sanctions is relatively small when state and local organizations are not treated as the restricted preserve of their immediate leaders. National party leaders ought to have access to party members everywhere as a normal and regular procedure because they share with local party leaders responsibility to the same party membership. It would always be proper for the national party leaders to discuss all party matters with the membership of any state or local party organization. Considering their great prestige, wise and able national party leaders will need very little more than this opportunity.

The political developments of our time place a heavy emphasis on national issues as the basis of party programs. As a result, the party membership is coming to look to the national party leaders for a larger role in intraparty affairs. There is some evidence of growing general agreement within the membership of each party, strong enough to form a basis of party unity, provided the parties maintain close contact with their own supporters.

In particular, *national party leaders have a legitimate interest in the nomination of congressional candidates,* though normally they try hard to avoid the appearance of any intervention. Depending on the circumstances, this interest can be expressed quite sufficiently by seeking a chance to discuss the nomination with the party membership in the congressional district. On the other hand, it should not be assumed that state and local party leaders usually have an interest in congressional nominations antagonistic to the interest of the national leaders in maintaining the general party policy. As a matter of fact, congressional nominations are not considered great prizes by the local party organization as generally as one might think. It is neglect of congressional nominations and elections more than any other factor that weakens party unity in Congress. It should be added, however, that what is said here about intraparty relations with respect to congressional nominations applies also to other party nominations.

The Inadequacy of the Existing Party System

The existing party system is inadequately prepared to meet the demands now being made upon it chiefly because its central institutions are not well organized to deal with national questions. The sort of party organization needed today is indirectly suggested by the origin of the traditional party structure. This structure developed in a period in which local interests were dominant and positive governmental action at the national level did not play the role it assumed later. . . .

SOME BASIC PROBLEMS

Party institutions and their operations cannot be divorced from the general conditions that govern the nature of the party system. Before we focus specifically on the deficiencies of existing party institutions, we must account for some of the more important factors that impress themselves upon both major parties.

What are the general features of party organization that have cast up continuing problems?

1. *The Federal Basis. The two parties are organized on a federal basis*, probably as a natural result of our federal type of government. In Charles E. Merriam's words, "The American party system has its roots in the states. Its regulation and control is conducted almost wholly, although not entirely, by the states acting separately." This means that *the national and state party organizations are largely independent of one another*, each operating within its own sphere, *without appreciable common approach to problems of party policy and strategy.*

Such independence has led to frequent and sharp differences between state and national organizations. Antagonisms are illustrated by such terms as national Republicans and Wisconsin Republicans, national Democrats and Dixiecrats. Moreover, state party organizations too often define their interests quite narrowly. This does not merely mean substantial disregard of national needs or matters of national interest, but it also means piecemeal as well as one-sided use of state power and state resources. As John M. Gaus has put it, "In many states—probably in almost all—the party systems are inadequate as instruments for reflecting the needs of our citizens for carefully thought-out, alternative programs of public housekeeping."

It is not being argued here that the party system should be cut free from its federal basis. Federalism is not a negative influence in itself; it is equally capable of positive accomplishments in the public interest. Whether it works in the one or the other direction depends in large part on how well the balance of forces within a federal organization accords with the needs of society. In the case of the American party system, *the real issue is not over the federal form of organization but over the right balance of forces within this type of organization.*

On that score, the party system is weighted much more heavily toward the state-local side than is true today of the federal system of government in the United States. The gap produces serious disabilities in government. It needs to be closed, even though obviously our traditions of localism, states rights and sectionalism will inevitably affect the pace of progress that can be expected.

A corollary of the kind of federalism now expressed in the party system is an excessive measure of internal separatism. The congressional party organization is independent of the national organization, and the House and Senate organizations of the same party are independent of each other. As a result, cooperation between these parts of the national party structure has not been easy to secure.

2. *The Location of Leadership.* In part because of the centrifugal drives that run through the party system, *party organization does not vest leadership of the party as a whole in either a single person or a committee.* The President, by virtue of his conspicuous position and

his real as well as symbolic role in public opinion, is commonly considered the leader of his party. If he has a vigorous personality and the disposition to press his views on party policy and strategy, he may become the actual leader during his presidential term. But even the President has no official position within the party organization, and his leadership is often resented and opposed. The presidential nominee of the defeated party is generally recognized as the "titular leader" of his party, yet the very title implies a lack of authority.

The National Chairman is most nearly in the top position, but if he tries to exercise initiative and leadership in matters other than the presidential campaign, his authority is almost certain to be challenged. Ill feeling, rather than harmony of policy and action, is likely to result. In sum, *there is at least no central figure or organ which could claim authority to take up party problems, policies and strategy.*

3. *The Ambiguity of Membership.* The vagueness of formal leadership that prevails at the top has its counterpart in the vagueness of formal membership at the bottom. *No understandings or rules or criteria exist with respect to membership in a party.* The general situation was well put by Senator Borah in a statement made in 1923:

> Any man who can carry a Republican primary is a Republican. He might believe in free trade, in unconditional membership in the League of Nations, in states' rights, and in every policy that the Democratic party ever advocated; yet, if he carried his Republican primary, he would be a Republican. He might go to the other extreme and believe in the communistic state, in the dictatorship of the proletariat, in the abolition of private property, and in the extermination of the bourgeoisie; yet, if he carried his Republican primary, he would still be a Republican.

It is obviously difficult, if not impossible, to secure anything like harmony of policy and action within political parties so loosely organized as this. On the other hand, it is easy to see that the voter's political choice when confined to candidates without a common bond in terms of program amounts to no more than taking a chance with an individual candidate. *Those who suggest that elections should deal with personalities but not with programs suggest at the same time that party membership should mean nothing at all.*

SPECIFIC DEFICIENCIES

So much for the most conspicuous consequences that stem from the general features of existing party organization. Now let us consider some more specific aspects pertinent to a reorganization of the national party structure.

1. *National Party Organs. The National Convention, as at present constituted and operated, is an unwieldly, unrepresentative and less than responsible body.* . . .

This lack of balance in representation, together with the peculiar atmosphere within which the Convention operates, makes it very hard for such a body to act in a deliberative and responsible manner. The moral authority of the National Convention to act in the name of the whole party would be greatly strengthened if more care were used to make the convention really representative of the party as a whole.

It can be said equally well of other institutions at the national level that they are not very well suited to carry today's burdens of an effective party system. *The National Committee is seldom a generally influential body and much less a working body.* Indeed, it rarely meets at all.

In *House and Senate,* the *campaign* committee of each party is concerned with aiding in the reelection of members of its chamber. These *committees do not always have a good working relationship with the National Committee.* They do not plan joint election strategy for both chambers and traditionally accept little responsibility for party leadership. Only in the past generation have the parties shown signs of developing a continuous working organization at the national level. *Although* their *interest in questions of party policy has grown, the national party organs are not so constituted nor so coordinated as to make it simple for them to pay enough attention to these questions.*

2. *Party Platforms.* The growing importance of national issues in American politics puts weight into the formulation of general statements of party policy. Of course, no single statement of party policy can express the whole program of the party in all of its particulars, including questions of timing. But it is obvious that a serious attempt to

define the propositions on which the parties intend to seek the voter's support would serve both party unity and party responsibility.

One of the reasons for the widespread lack of respect for party platforms is that they have seldom been used by the parties to get a mandate from the people. By and large, *alternatives between the parties are defined so badly that it is often difficult to determine what the election has decided even in broadest terms.* Yet unused resources are available to the parties in the democratic process itself if they learn to use a statement of policy as the basis for the election campaign. Platforms acquire authority when they are so used.

The prevailing procedure for the writing and adoption of national party platforms is too hurried and too remote from the process by which actual decisions are made to command the respect of the whole party and the electorate. The drafting of a platform ought to be the work of months, not of a day or two; it ought to be linked closely with the formulation of party policy as a continuing activity. Party policy—in its bricks and straws—is made, applied, explored and tested in congressional and presidential decisions, in the executive departments, in the work of research staffs, in committee hearings, and in congressional debates. No party convention can pull a party program out of the air. *The platform should be the end product of a long search for a working agreement within the party.*

3. *Intraparty Democracy.* One of the principal functions of the parties—in terms of the concept of party we elaborated in the preceding section—is to extend to the fullest the citizen's participation in public affairs. Measured by this standard, the existing parties are painfully deficient. Direct primary legislation offers opportunities for the creation of a broad base on which to build the party structure, but these opportunities have rarely been fully utilized.

Too little consideration has been given to ways and means of bringing about a constructive relationship between the party and its members. Indeed, any organization really concerned about this relationship does a multitude of things that American parties generally do not do to maintain close contact with the membership. Party membership ought to become a year-round matter, both with constructive activities by the members and with mechanisms by which the party organizations can absorb the benefits of wider political participation. . . .

New Demands Upon Party Leadership

THE NATURE OF MODERN PUBLIC POLICY

1. *Broad Range of Policy. The expanding responsibilities of modern government have brought about so extensive an interlacing of governmental action with the country's economic and social life that the need for coordinated and coherent programs, legislative as well as administrative, has become paramount.* Formulating and executing such general programs involves more than technical knowledge. *In a democracy no general program can be adopted and carried out without wide political support.* Support must be strong enough and stable enough to guard the program as far as possible against such drives as come forth constantly from a multitude of special interests seeking their own ends. This kind of political support can be mobilized on a continuing basis only by stronger parties.

Broad governmental programs need to be built on a foundation of political commitments as written into the programs of adequately organized parties. This is true today also of governmental programs erected on bipartisan backing. In that respect the political requirements to sustain American diplomacy are very different from those of the period before World War I, for example. As Walter Lippmann has recently written of the requirements of bipartisan foreign policy, "It takes two organized parties, each with its recognized leaders in the field of foreign affairs. Today neither party is organized. Neither party has leaders in the field of foreign affairs. In this chaos no Secretary of State can function successfully."

2. *Impact on the Public.* What is said here about the need for an adequate political base for foreign policy applies equally to such other large sectors of public concern as national defense and economic pol-

icy. In each area, the problems are so interrelated that the activities of the government must be integrated over a very wide front. *In a predominantly industrial society, public policy tends to be widely inclusive, involving in its objectives and effects very large segments of the public or even the whole country.* ...

RISE OF NATION-WIDE POLICY ISSUES

1. *An Historic Trend.* Even if the international scene did not look as it does, *the changes in the nature and scope of public policy* here indicated would press upon the political process. For they *are the result of changes in the social structure and the economy of the United States.* The long-range transformations expressed in industrialization and urbanization and the revolution in transportation and communication were bound to create a truly national economy and to affect significantly the bases of American politics. ...

2. *Past and Present Factors.* It is much the same thing to say that *there has been in recent decades a continuing decline of sectionalism,* first noted by Arthur N. Holcombe nearly twenty years ago. Statistical evidence such as is available for the last generation shows that the most significant political trends in the country have been national, not sectional or local. This is not to say that sectionalism is likely to drop to insignificance as a factor in American politics. Here as elsewhere in the political system, change is a matter of degree. The relative decline of the strength of sectional alignments is nevertheless a matter of great consequence. Elections are increasingly won and lost by influences felt throughout the land.

The measurable shift from sectional to national politics cannot fail to have a corresponding effect on party organization and the locus of power within the parties. *Party organization designed to deal with the increasing volume of national issues must give wider range to the national party leadership.* ...

3. *New Interest Groups in Politics. The economic and social factors that have reduced the weight of sectionalism have also resulted in the development of a new type of interest group, built upon large*

membership. These new interest groups, found principally in the areas of industrial labor and agriculture, are pursuing a novel political strategy. *To a much greater extent than in the past, they operate as if they were auxiliary organizations of one or the other party.* The growing conversion of most of the labor movement to party action is a case in point. Labor organizations now participate energetically in election contests. They register voters, take part in the nominating process, raise campaign funds, issue campaign literature and perform other functions once on the whole reserved for the parties.

Thus the old local monopolies of the regular party organizations have been broken by new large-membership groups. To a very considerable extent the regular party organizations are now so yoked into a partnership with the newcomers that they have lost much of their old freedom of action. The successful political leader in the future is likely to be one who is skillful in maintaining a good working alliance between the older and the newer types of political organization. This applies partly even to conditions today.

The emphasis of the new large-membership organizations is on national rather than sectional issues. What is no less significant, the interests of the membership are not identified with any single product or commodity. Farmers, for instance, cannot hope to prosper in an ailing economy. Workers must measure their pay against the level of prices as well as the value of social security. Hence the large-membership groups are inevitably pushed into consideration of all the factors that affect the national well-being. How parties stand on programs designed to bring about stability and healthy expansion in the economy as a whole is therefore of great concern to most of the new groups in American politics.

The Question of Constitutional Amendment

1. *A Cabinet System?* It is altogether clear that party responsibility cannot be legislated into being. Not a few Americans have argued,

however, that something like the British system of responsible cabinet government would have to be grafted to ours before an effective party system could come about in the United States. Usually this idea takes the form of proposals to amend the Constitution to give the President the right to dissolve Congress and to call a new election at any time, besides certain other changes in the Constitution.

A responsible cabinet system makes the leaders of the majority party in the legislature the heads of the executive departments, *collectively accountable* to their own legislative majority *for the conduct of the government*. Such a relationship prompts close cooperation between the executive and legislative branches. The legislative majority of the cabinet forms a party team which as such can readily be held responsible for its policies. This governmental system is built around the parties, which play the key role in it.

2. *Strong Parties as a Condition.* We do not here need to take a position on the abstract merits of the cabinet system. On the question whether it could be successfully fitted into the American scheme of congressional-presidential government, opinions are widely divided. Even if it were conceded to be desirable *to amend the Constitution in order to create a responsible cabinet system,* it should be plain that this *is not a practicable way of getting more effective parties*. Such an amendment, if it offered likelihood of being adopted at all, would make sense only when the parties have actually demonstrated the strength they now lack. When they show that strength, a constitutional amendment to achieve this end would be unnecessary.

On the other hand, the experience of foreign countries suggests that adoption of the cabinet system does not automatically result in an effective party system. Cabinet systems differ in their results and affect the party system in different ways. Moreover, it is easy to overestimate not only the expected benefits of a constitutional amendment but also the rigidity of the existing constitutional arrangements in the United States. Certainly the roles of the President and Congress are defined by the Constitution in terms that leave both free to cooperate and to rely on the concept of party responsibility.

3. *Adaptation within the Constitution. The parties can do much to*

adapt the usages under the Constitution to their purposes. When strong enough, the parties obviously can furnish the President and Congress a political basis of cooperation within the Constitution as it stands today.

Actually the parties have not carefully explored the opportunities they have for more responsible operation under existing constitutional arrangements. It is logical first to find out what can be done under present conditions to invigorate the parties before accepting the conclusion that action has to begin with changing a constitutional system that did not contemplate the growing need for party responsibility when it was set up.

PRESSURE GROUPS AND LOBBIES

The following selection, from a classic government report, highlights the problem of special interest or pressure group politics. Unlike the political party which seeks to control the administration of the government, the pressure group, which usually represents a single interest (e.g., natural gas producers or real estate operators), is organized to influence the shaping of government policies in its behalf, generally by promoting or retarding legislation affecting its interest. The lobby, or organization that politicks for the group, is an integral part of the democratic process protected by the First Amendment. However, the strongest lobbies, representing the greatest private economic power, shape public policy in a way that frequently damages the public interest which, more often than not, transcends group lines or is unrepresented by lobbies. The Federal Lobbying Act of 1946, which is not regulatory, merely requires lobbies to register and disclose expenses, but is so full of loopholes that many of the most powerful lobbies either do not register or report only expenses "directly" calculated to influence legislation. Multimillion-dollar propaganda campaigns and other "indirect" expenses are not disclosed. In the absence of responsible and disciplined parties, lobbies, which are not subject to the electoral process, can thwart or pervert the general welfare.

$\mathcal{T}$ H E American people are confronted with the problem of who shall control the Government, by what means, and to what ends.

Since the founding of the Republic, the governmental process has been characterized by a struggle for control. With increasing stresses and strains as a result of internal maladjustments and foreign war, the struggle has taken on new and vital significance.

Control Versus Power

Governmental power is qualitatively different from control. Power is a political term, synonymous with authority. Control is dynamic and constantly seeks new methods of limiting or using power. Government may possess power and at the same time wield control, as in a totalitarian state; but ordinarily, in a democracy, power resides in the government, while control is exercised by the various pressure groups, chief of which is business. The extent of the Government's control is limited, not only by the Constitution but by our traditional belief that government should not "compete" with business but should act merely as an umpire in the struggle for control. Only in comparatively recent times, under stress of depression and greatly accelerated technological change, has this traditional belief yielded ground to the idea of increased government activity.

The role of business, on the other hand, has never been static. From the beginning, business has been intent upon wielding economic power and, when necessary, political control for its own purpose. The purpose, moreover, is not solely profit, but includes the exercise of control per se, as an attribute of ownership.

Even today, when the purposeful use of government power for the general welfare is more widely accepted than at any time in our history, government does not begin to approach the fusion of power and will characteristic of business.

Temporary National Economic Committee, *Investigation of Concentration of Economic Power. Monograph No. 26: Economic Power and Political Pressures*, Senate Committee Print, 76th Congress, 3rd session (Washington: G.P.O., 1941), pp. 1-10, 47-56, *passim*.

The Contestants

But economic power and political power are general terms. To understand them it is necessary to determine who uses them, how, for what purposes, and with what results.

Government itself is both a form of power and a situs of control. Government in a democracy, however, does not act independently of the electorate; nor does our Federal Government as now constituted proceed in a logical way toward the attainment of carefully thought out and consistent goals.

In the first place, our Government is established on a geographical basis of representation. State, county, and district lines provide an easy way of securing representation, but the assumption that people living in a certain area on the map share, even in a general way, the interests of their neighbors is unjustified, if not actually false. Also, political representation is generally secured through the party system, and as such represents a compromise at the outset. A party platform, adopted to appeal to as large a sector of the electorate as possible, cannot follow completely the interests of any group. Lip service, at least, must be paid to the complex of interests represented in the community.

The relatively short time served by public officials is also a limiting factor on the effectiveness of government control. . . .

Philosophically, also, government is amorphous. Within broad limits there are nearly as many philosophies of government as there are men in it, while pressure groups have a tremendous unifying principle in the mere fact of their organization about a certain concept. Congressmen act in a multiple capacity, reflecting at different times a functional, sectional, personal, or partisan viewpoint, but with a few major exceptions, such as the Social Security Act and certain labor legislation, they appear to respond more readily to pressure from business than from other groups. There is probably a far greater difference in ideology between a high-tariff, industrialist Congressman from Massachusetts and a public ownership advocate from the Middle or Far West than there is between two members of the National Association of Manufacturers, or two members of the National Grange. The latter have at least a common economic interest, while the former are probably poles apart on most of the questions which they are called upon to decide.

While the business community may, on occasion, elect "its man" to Congress or to the Presidency, or secure his appointment to a governmental office or to the courts, its indirect influence is of far greater importance. Pressure groups generally find it more satisfactory to influence the votes of legislators in their behalf than to try to elect their own representatives to office. . . .

Economic power is rather widely diffused, although its control is concentrated, as pointed out above. In the struggle for dominance, it is exerted largely through pressure groups—groups organized for the purpose of applying political and economic pressure to secure their own ends. It is these pressure groups with which this study is largely concerned. By far the largest and most important of these groups is to be found in "business," which in this study means the business community, as dominated by the 200 largest nonfinancial and the 50 largest financial corporations, and the employer and trade associations into which it and its satellites are organized. These 250 corporations represent a concentration of economic power in the fields of manufacturing, transportation, electric and gas utilities, and mining, and, to a lesser extent, merchandising, the service industries, and even agriculture.

Another large segment of pressure groups includes the patriotic and service organizations, such as the Daughters of the American Revolution, the American Legion, the Veterans of Foreign Wars, the Navy League, etc.

A third segment includes the reform groups—the Women's Christian Temperance Union, the National Civil Service Reform League, the League of Women Voters, etc.

The farm groups include the National Grange, the American Farm Bureau Federation, and the Farmers' Educational and Cooperative Union, along with minor groups like the Tenants' and Sharecroppers' Union.

There are numerous labor groups, the most powerful being the

American Federation of Labor, the Congress of Industrial Organizations, and the various railway brotherhoods. . . .

This enumeration by no means includes all the pressure groups.
Some of them spring up for immediate purposes, and when those purposes are achieved disappear. Some of them are organized for purposes other than the wielding of political and economic power, and
adopt that function only temporarily. The American Association of
University Women is such an organization, which is politically active
only on sporadic occasions.

A number of groups organized for the preservation of civil rights,
the advancement of democracy, or for purely humanitarian motives,
such as the American Civil Liberties Union, the National Association
for the Advancement of Colored People, the various committees for
the aid of refugees, or for Spain or China, the Red Cross, etc., should
also be classified separately. They are normally active only for their
own purposes, and do not lend themselves readily to alliances with
other groups, except to the extent to which their membership is active
politically.

There is another contestant in the struggle for power which cannot
be ignored, although it is customarily treated by the pressure groups
more as an instrument for securing and maintaining their own control
than as a rival in the contest. This is the general public. The public is
an amorphous mass, largely directionless, often easily swayed, gullible, and easily misled. Nevertheless, it possesses a tremendous
potential strength and an enormous determination when it finds a
channel for its energies. It would be a mistake to underrate mass
opinion, however futile it may seem at any particular moment to try
to goad it into effective action in its own behalf.

Mass opinion sets the stage for political action at any particular
moment in this country, to a large degree. Gullible as it is, it cannot
in ordinary times be pushed beyond a certain point. It is utterly impossible to return to the political conditions of 1800, or 1910, or even
1930, partly because economic conditions have changed and partly
because it is impossible to set back the clock of public opinion. The
gradual extension of suffrage, unionization, popular control of legis-

lation, extension of social services—all these things are now in the realm of public policy and cannot be removed except by a violent revolution and the use of unexampled force. Even then, most of them would be retained.

Pressure groups attempt to mold public opinion to accomplish their own aims, and at any given moment it seems that government is the result of a compromise between conflicting pressure groups. . . .

Methods of Controlling Power

The methods by which control of power is sought are as varied as the groups which seek it. The role of the general public in the contest may to a large extent be ignored, since the public is generally too formless, too inchoate, to apply pressure at given points for a given purpose, and is largely the passive instrument which both business and government use to strengthen their own arms.

Our purpose is to discover the techniques by which power is directed by conflicting forces toward the attainment of specific goals. The chief contestants in this conflict are business and government. Government, usually in response to external stimuli, seeks to expand its functions, to put itself on an equal footing with business. Business seeks to hold back the rising tide of government activity, struggling to keep itself free from government regulation, so as to pursue its own ends unhampered. Both argue that they work in the interest of the general welfare.

While there has been some interest in this country in favor of government ownership of economic enterprises, it is a philosophy which has never been adopted as a program of action by any large group. The expansion of government activity has been along the lines of providing social services favorable to many groups which would otherwise not be furnished at all, and of regulating economic activity in the public interest.

Business, on the other hand, has fought such regulation and the expansion of social services, and even more bitterly has fought the idea of government ownership. The fight occurs largely in the political arena, but it does not end with the election of Congressmen and Senators. Election is but one phase of the process. The selection of candidates, the drafting of platforms, the party caucus, all function largely in advance of the legislative process. Pressures on Congress while legislating and appropriating, manipulation of law enforcement and administration, and use of the judicial process to achieve individual or group ends, take place during or after the legislative process.

Through the press, public opinion, and pressure groups it is possible to influence the political process. While all three of these factors have played a part in the process since our beginnings as a nation, the extent and consciousness of their use has grown inordinately. They are employed by all contestants in the struggle for control, but reflect the viewpoint of business more accurately than that of others. The press today is not the same kind of factor in the political process that it was in Thomas Jefferson's day. Although the economic basis of politics today is in many respects similar to that outlined by Madison in the Federalist, today's economic pressure groups have advantages which Madison never dreamed of. The revolution in communications, produced by American ingenuity and promoted by American business, makes the press, the radio, and other opinion-forming instruments far more important in the political process than ever before. Both press and radio are, after all, "big business," and even when they possess the highest integrity, they are the prisoners of their own beliefs.

The development of the corporation as a means of control of property necessitates ranking it, too, as an important factor in the political process. By means of the private corporation, ownership of much of American business property has been separated from effective control of that property. Ownership is diffused, at least to some extent; control is concentrated. This development is so recent (it has occurred within the last two decades or so) that its effect on the working of our governmental institutions cannot yet be accurately evaluated. Enough is known, however, to justify the statement that it is warping the basic concepts of our Government. Extending beyond State lines in great national economic empires, business corporations have grown greater than the States which created them. By insisting on the principle of federalism—the division of power between the States and the Federal Government—as a basic tenet in our political philosophy, corporations have been able in large measure to limit the strength of the political power which might control them.

Characteristics of the Struggle

Among the noteworthy characteristics of the struggle for power between government and business are—

1. The invisibility of most of the action.
2. The continuity of the struggle.
3. Its varying intensity.
4. Its constantly shifting battleground.

INVISIBILITY

Although any legislation under consideration in Congress is spotlighted in the daily news, although the President's activities and the administrative decisions of the various Government agencies are frequently headlined in press and radio, and although court decisions are a matter of widespread public interest, still it is true that a large, and extremely important, part of the governmental process is hidden from the public.

It is a commonplace that the work of Congress is done not in the Senate and House chambers, where the spectators come to watch, but in the committee rooms of the congressional committees. Even this, however, is but a faint indication of the extent to which governmental activity is carried on behind the scenes. The factors which influence legislators are only rarely the opinions of their colleagues, uttered in formal debate in Congress. They are the legislator's own political convictions, his mail from his district or State, the lobbyists who approach him in his office or in the halls of the Capitol, or the witnesses who appear before him in committee. None of these activities is carried on with the publicity devoted to formal congressional action. The callers at the White House rarely are even listed in the papers, although one or two Washington papers make a habit of printing the day's appointments. Still less are callers upon department administrators listed. The trade journal of a certain industry group may mention that its members went to Washington on a mission of benefit to the industry, but the news does not get into the general press. Letters, telegrams, telephone calls, personal visits, and the other contacts between contestants are rarely of enough immediate dramatic content to secure public attention, even if it were not usually made a point to conduct such activities without publicity.

Another strong reason for this invisibility is to be found in the geographical basis of legislative and judicial representation. This organization of government obscures the economic or functional basis for legislative decisions, which are frequently far more compelling than a geographical accident. The political process is invisible also because citizen groups, the most energetic and purposeful of the working forces of government, are completely unprovided for by the written Constitution. Only in the living Constitution are they recognized as having significance along with the formal Government agencies. They function in and through the Government structure, without, however, as a rule suffering from the white light of publicity which surrounds it. . . .

THE SITE OF THE CONFLICT

At what point the brunt of the battle is borne depends on a number of factors, at any particular time. It depends, among other things, on the nature and number of current issues, upon the personnel of the government agencies, Congress, or the Supreme Court, or upon the trend of dominant public opinion.

The first battle of the conflict occurs in the choice of legislators. The second takes place in the legislature itself. If business loses that, it resorts to the administrative agencies charged with the enforcement of the law; if it loses there, or sometimes while it is fighting there, it has recourse to the courts; and if it loses again, the struggle reverts to the legislature, taking the form of an attempt to amend or repeal the law. The forces of propaganda are, of course, in constant use. Business, for instance, first sought to defeat the National Labor Relations Act in Congress. Failing that, a number of trade journals, the publications of the National Association of Manufacturers and the United States Chamber of Commerce recommended that the act be ignored until it was tested in the courts. (At that time, it seemed likely that a favorable court decision could be secured.) When the act was finally declared constitutional, however, the focus of the attack shifted first to the approaching congressional elections, in the hope of amending the act, and then to Congress itself.

Although by no means always favorable, the circumstances determining the site of the struggle usually favor business. Business is less restricted than government in choosing the place to fight. It can fight or not, secure in its conviction that "sixty billion dollars can't be wrong." If it feels itself compelled to fight it can accept the challenge, at the same time starting a back fire elsewhere.

In this connection the business orientation of the newspaper press is a valuable asset. In the nature of . . . things, public opinion is usually well disposed toward business. This is a natural consequence of the popular belief in the virtues of the American system, as understood by the business community. Business is more or less unconsciously assumed to be right. Government is the "prosecutor." But, in addition, newspapers have it in their power materially to influence public opinion on particular issues. When it comes to measuring particular situations of fact against general principles and presenting the comparison as news, newspapers are shapers of opinion as well as purveyors of fact. Editors are aware of this, of course, and many take special precautions to avoid it. With others, editorializing is practiced as a matter of course. And even where editors and publishers are men of the highest integrity, they are owners and managers of big business enterprises, and their papers inevitably reflect, at least to some extent, their economic interest. When organized business deliberately propagandizes the country, using newspaper advertising as one medium, the press is a direct means of channeling business views into the public mind.

Slogans and clichés have a special importance in rendering favorable the circumstances in which business chooses to stand against government. "Inalienable rights," "individual initiative and effort," "private ownership and control" are typical of those used by the National Association of Manufacturers. They are among the essential features of the "American System." They constitute the description of the economy which business prefers, but they seem to hark back to the days before the emergence of the modern corporation as a dominant institution. . . .

Language used by Thomas Jefferson to state the relationship between citizens and government necessary for the development of the individual personality, has been used by business to attract public support in its effort to avoid regulation. The law, the newspaper press, and the advertising profession have all helped business by spreading this changed conception of the Jeffersonian idea. . . .

Political Pressure Groups

The constituent groups into which politically active Americans are divided have as their practical objective the favorable consideration of their respective aims by the legislative, executive, and judicial branches of the Government. We have seen how pressure groups, by soliciting general approval for their aims, raise them to the status of public problems. Also, we have considered the role of these groups in the manufacture of public opinion. It is now appropriate to scrutinize more closely the place of pressure groups in American political life.

Their goal is Government sanction of their continually emerging demands. Those demands are insistent no matter what the form of organization of the group. Trade associations and organizations of professional people press their demands unhindered on the formal agencies of the Government. Similarly, groupings of industrialists and federations of labor and veterans' units insist on consideration of their desires. Peace and patriotic-minded societies likewise impress their programs on the formally-selected officials of the Government. Added together, these citizen groups of varied shape constitute a sizable portion of the American people. And, what is more important, they include practically all the people who recognize the value of official consideration of private interests and are so situated as to command that consideration. . . .

The Lobby and Its Technique

From this broad statement on pressure groups, let us proceed to a closer examination of lobby technique in general.

In their search for governmental favors, national associations of citizens all conform to a pattern which is more or less standardized. They maintain lobbies at Washington, of varying size and resources. The lobby of the United States Chamber of Commerce, for example, is a department of the national headquarters and is maintained on an impressive scale. In contrast is the single lobbyist of the Women's International League for Peace and Freedom.

Some lobbies are permanent, others intermittent or temporary. Important citizen groups organized nationally maintain permanent lobbies. Others maintain intermittent lobbies which have been effective in legislative matters, such as the Fair Trade League, with its objective of retail price fixing. The American Bar Association's special representative in Washington during the fight on President Roosevelt's Supreme Court reorganization proposal is an example of a temporary lobby. At a minimum, each lobby usually includes a legislative agent and a staff of research workers.

It is the lobbyist's job to put on the statute books the bills which embody the aims of his association, or of which it approves, and to keep off the statute books those bills of which it disapproves. Consequently, it is the desire of the typical national association to build a bloc of votes in Congress and then to back it at the right junctures with pressure from the country. The pressure is exerted on neutral or unsympathetic Congressmen by the association's Nation-wide membership, as an adjunct of a favorable, or at least not hostile, public mood built up by the association's active propaganda.

The services which a bloc of votes in Congress can render a national association are numerous and valuable. Obviously the most valuable is frankly to represent the citizen group in Congress. Possibly the best known example of such occupational representation by geographically-elected representatives is the farm bloc, which was founded by the Farm Bureau Federation in 1921 and held the balance of power in the Sixty-sixth and Sixty-seventh Congresses. For a group to be able thus to rely on some definite support is always worth a great deal.

In addition to being ready to vote for the group's bills, there are many ways in which a bloc may render service to the group. Sympathetic legislators can watch and influence committee appointments, and can urge committee members to report out bills. Members of the bloc can speak for the group on the floor of the House or Senate. They can introduce bills. Moreover, any member of the bloc can use his franking privilege to send association propaganda through the mails free of postal charge. This propaganda takes the form either of a Member's speech on the piece of legislation in question, or of a prepared statement inserted in the Record through "leave to print." These are all normal and time-honored methods by which sympathetic blocs in Congress can advance the aims of citizen groups.

With several hundred nationally organized citizen groups with agents in Washington, it is obvious that only a relatively small number can gain control of congressional blocs. For representation before Congress, most of the groups must rely primarily on their legislative agents. Even those supported by congressional blocs lean heavily on their lobbyists. In fact, the lobbyist is the key factor in pressure politics. On him rests the responsibility not only of translating his association's legislative program into law as fast as possible, but also of thwarting legislation running counter to that program.

This means that the alert lobbyist must interest himself in a wide variety of subjects on which Congress acts. The objectives of some groups are few and specific, and their lobbyists accordingly need pay but little attention to other legislative proposals. Other groups, however, aim at general objectives, which, to be reached and held, require legislative action in a dozen fields. Outstanding among such groups are those including the Nation's laborers, businessmen, manufacturers; its transport and public utility systems; its bankers, farmers, and professional people. The lobbyists who guard the interests of these groups in Washington must scrutinize carefully a bewildering array of bills. Tax measures and appropriations need close examination. Bills providing for Government reorganization must also be studied.

For almost all these groups the prospects of reaching their objectives are dimmed or brightened by existing and proposed laws dealing with natural resources, transportation facilities, manufacturing, processing, grades and standards, and distribution; with marketing and trading, foreign commerce, banking and credit, and postal operations, quarantine and sanitary measures, and trade practices; with Government purchasing, roads, local tax systems, and education. Almost every one of these subjects, therefore, falls within the scope of the lobbyist's concern. Both his own personal success and that of his association's program depend on his ability to win battles on this many-sided legislative front. . . .

The lobbyist or his witnesses explains to Members of Congress why the attainment of the aim depends upon the enactment of many specific bills and why the general welfare will be promoted by the bills in which he is interested. Part of the lobbyist's job is to make Congress feel that the "public" is back of the bills which his association wants passed. "The men who seek special favors of Congress * * * do not bribe, or give free passes, or pay election expenses; they attempt to make the legislators think that the thing they want is the thing that the public wants." In this process of identifying group interest with public interest the lobbyist occupies the key position.

Congress is importuned for special favors not only by lobbyists who work openly in Washington, but also by pressure exerted from behind the scenes. The pressure reaches a Congressman through telegrams, resolutions, letters, and delegations of constituents, all urging him to vote thus-and-so on a particular bill. The constituents who exert this sort of pressure are not limited to members of the association whose lobbyist directs the campaign. They include also those of many other groups—political clubs, chambers of commerce, young voters' leagues, independent citizens' alliances, etc. Thus a lobbyist mobilizes behind a measure support from a dozen or more different quarters in a congressional district.

Once the decision is made by the officials of the association interested in the bill to "turn the heat on Congress," a number of district organizers tour the country, contacting local organization secretaries, ambitious young lawyers and professional men, and local celebrities for the purpose of starting the avalanche of letters and telegrams speeding toward the Capitol. Meanwhile, in Washington, the lobbyist is acting as coordinator of the field armies. . . . The whole strategy of his movements is to stay out of the limelight and to let the voters speak to their Congressmen for him.

On occasion Congressmen are appealed to through this method to vote against a bill because it is "communistic" or "socialistic." In such cases the lobbyist's aim is to have the pressure come to Members of Congress from one or more patriotic organizations. . . .

Devious as well as direct methods are thus employed by lobbyists to influence Congress. To oppose legislation because it is communistic or socialistic and, therefore, un-American, is to take a stand on generalities which is, nevertheless, unassailable, when love of America stands highest in the scale of popular loyalties. . . .

These special-interest groups are not limited by the boundaries of congressional districts. Puzzled by problems beyond their abilities to solve and, turning to the Government for help, they have discovered that the system of representation in Congress makes no provision for them. Two-party government discourages their entrance into politics, thus forcing them into extra-legal channels to achieve their aims in the sphere of legislative activity. The means which they have evolved to do this is the lobby, which thus becomes an instrument not only of opinion forming, but of providing functional, nongeographic interests with representation at Washington.

The decline of the political party as a leader in opinion has been accompanied by the rise of these organized groups of voters. Obviously, the effect of this shift in the relative importance of the party in the political process is important. It has resulted in the virtual domination of politics by the citizen group movement. Both during and after elections the groups hold the key to the explanation of much party behavior. As leaders in the formation of opinion, the parties at election time seek their support more assiduously than that of aggregates of individuals. In election campaigns this means that the real significance of the platform on which party nominees run for election can be found only in the stated or implied desires of the groups supporting the candidates. "The voice which political parties hear now is the voice of groups rather than that of political leaders who profess to speak for the people."

The range of that voice extends to Washington as well. Partisans in Congress and administration also listen to group opinion. Members of Congress are elected by parties but in their votes they tend to respond as a rule more to the voice of groups than to that of the party....

Control of legislation and offices has thus shifted in large measure from the parties to the lobbies and allied organizations.

The real danger of this situation lies not in functional or group representation before Congress, but in the possibility that Congress will be swayed by a pressure out of proportion to the actual number of people in the group, or without regard to the effect of the legislation on the general public. To a certain extent the parties themselves are a check on this dangerous tendency....

While this may be too optimistic an appraisal of the situation, it is still true that, without the support of the leaders of the majority party in Congress, citizen groups usually are not able to enforce their demands.

Both parties and groups are active in the shaping of policy. Through nominations of personable candidates, bargains with citizen groups and political factions, and success in elections, the parties play the dominant role in the determination of broad policy. At the same time, the substance of policy both in the beginning and as revised through the years is due more to pressure groups. . . . The competition among groups for official approval of their aims is perhaps the outstanding characteristic of the governmental process in America of the twentieth century.

RACES WITHOUT VOTES

Government by consent of the governed, based on the freedom of citizens to make and enforce their own laws through elected representatives, depends upon the "right" to vote. Racial discrimination at the polls, although unconstitutional and indefensible, is widespread in the black belt areas of the South, with the result that Negro citizens, deprived of representation, are victimized by public policy and degraded as human beings. The following selection from the recent report on voting, by the United States Commission on Civil Rights, objectively describes the chasm between American principles and daily practices.

$\mathcal{N}$ INE years ago the Department of Justice prepared a brief history of protection of constitutional rights of individuals during the preceding 20 years. On the right to vote, this report stated: "In 1932, the question as to the right of Negroes to vote involved 12 Southern States—Alabama, Arkansas, Florida, Georgia, Louisiana, Mississippi, North Carolina, Oklahoma, South Carolina, Tennessee, Texas, and Virginia." Apparently, even at that time, Negroes had no difficulty in registering and voting in the majority of our States.

The accuracy of this conclusion is borne out by the experience of the Commission on Civil Rights in the brief span of its operations. Although the Commission has received 382 sworn complaints from persons alleging that they had been denied the right to vote or to have their vote counted by reason of race, color, religion, or national origin,

1961 United States Commission on Civil Rights Report (Washington: G.P.O., 1961), vol. 1, *Voting*, pp. 21-22, 29-30, 111-112.

with the exception of three complaints from New York, all such complaints originated from Southern States mentioned in the Department of Justice's report. (The complaints from New York involved Puerto Rican American citizens who, although literate in Spanish, could not satisfy the English literacy test of that State.) Nor has other evidence of racial discrimination in voting in any of the other 37 States come to the Commission's attention.

In 1960, Negroes constituted 10.5 percent of the total U.S. population—18,871,831 out of 179,323,175 persons. Negro population throughout the 50 States and the District of Columbia varied from a low of one-tenth of 1 percent in both North Dakota and Vermont to a high of 53.9 percent in the District of Columbia, with a majority (53 percent) living in the 12 Southern States mentioned above. Thus in 1960, 47 percent of all Negro American citizens resided in 38 States which had no recent history of discriminatory denials of the right to vote.

In 1932, "In these [12 Southern] States, Negroes were so effectively disfranchised, regardless of the 14th and 15th amendments to the Constitution, that considerably fewer than a hundred thousand were able to vote in general election[s] and virtually none was permitted to vote in the primary election[s]." However this situation had drastically altered by 1952.

The most important change, accomplished through private lawsuits, was the virtual elimination of "white primaries" in 1944. A second significant change was voluntary State action abolishing the poll tax as a prerequisite for voting: Louisiana in 1934, Florida in 1937, Georgia in 1945, South Carolina in 1951, and Tennessee in 1953. Today, only five Southern States—Alabama, Mississippi, Arkansas, Texas, and Virginia—still require payment of poll tax as a prerequisite for voting.

By 1947, when the number of voting-age Negroes in the 12 Southern States was 5,069,805, the number of registered Negroes had risen from 100,000 in 1932 to 645,000; by 1952, this number exceeded 1 million. Today, there are 5,131,042 nonwhites of voting age in these 12 States, of whom a total of 1,361,944 are registered to vote.

The Commission's investigations and studies since 1957 indicate that discriminatory disfranchisement no longer exists in all of the 12 Southern States. The Commission used four principal criteria to determine the presence of discriminatory disfranchisement: (1) sworn complaints to the Commission; (2) actions instituted by the Department of Justice pursuant to the new civil remedies of the Civil Rights Acts of 1957 and 1960; (3) private-party litigation to secure the right to vote; and (4) the lack of any registered Negroes, or minimal Negro registration, in counties where there is a substantial Negro population. The absence of complaints to the Commission, actions by the Department of Justice, private litigation, or other indications of discrimination, have led the Commission to conclude that, with the possible exception of a deterrent effect of the poll tax—which does not appear generally to be discriminatory upon the basis of race or color—Negroes now appear to encounter no significant racially motivated impediments to voting in 4 of the 12 Southern States: Arkansas, Oklahoma, Texas, and Virginia.

In 1961, then, the problem of denials of the right to vote because of race appears to occur in only eight Southern States—Alabama, Florida, Georgia, Louisiana, Mississippi, North Carolina, South Carolina, and Tennessee—in which less than 40 percent of the total Negro population resides. Even in these 8 States, however, with a total of 3,737,242 nonwhites of voting age, some 1,014,454 nonwhites are registered to vote. Moreover, discrimination against Negro suffrage does not appear to prevail in every county in any of these States. The Commission has found that in Florida, North Carolina, and Tennessee, it is limited to only a few isolated counties. Although arbitrary denial of the right to vote is more widespread in the remaining five States, there too it exists on something like a "local option" basis.

This is not to say that exclusion of Negroes from the suffrage, however local, is not a matter of national concern. Toleration of even a single instance of such practice constitutes a partial repudiation of our faith in the democratic system. Nevertheless, it seems worthwhile to point out that the majority of Negro American citizens do not now suffer discriminatory denial of their right to vote.

While the Commission's studies do not allow a definitive statement as to the number of counties where discrimination is present—or the number where it is absent—they do indicate that there are about 100 counties in the 8 Southern States mentioned in which there is reason to believe that substantial discriminatory disfranchisement of Negroes still exists. . . .

Georgia

The Negro's voting status in Georgia varies from holding the balance of political power, as in Fulton County (Atlanta), to total exclusion from the suffrage in some rural counties. While the Commission has yet to receive a sworn voting complaint from Georgia, this cannot, unfortunately, be taken to show a lack of racial discrimination in the State.

TERRELL COUNTY

Terrell County, scene of the first court action brought under the Civil Rights Act of 1957, is situated in southwest Georgia. A suit filed by the Department of Justice in September of 1958 went to trial in 1960 after a ruling unfavorable to the Government had been reversed by the Supreme Court. After trial, the U.S. district court found that although six Negro applicants (two held master's degrees, two bachelor's degrees, and one had had 1 year of college training) "read intelligibly, the board of registrars determined that [five] read unintelligibly and denied their applications"; that although the sixth "was both willing and able to write any section of the Constitution of the State of Georgia or of the United States legibly upon dictation . . . defendant Raines dictated at such speed as to make it impossible [for him] . . . to correctly write all that defendant Raines dictated." Upon this "pretended basis of failure," the Board denied his application. The district court, on September 13, 1960, found that 30 named Negroes had been subjected to "distinctions in the registration process on the basis of their race and color"; it ordered the names of 4 Negroes put on the rolls, and issued an injunction against further discriminatory conduct.

LEE COUNTY

This county, adjacent to Terrell, was surveyed as part of the Commission's black belt study. In 1958, 29 Negroes were registered; in 1960, although there were 1,795 Negroes of voting age, all persons interviewed by the Commission agreed that the number registered was less than 29. The Negro informants attributed this to fear of economic reprisals—loss of jobs, and refusal to gin cotton, or purchase other crops—and threat of physical violence. The whites interviewed denied that this was true and both white and Negro interviewees blamed Negro illiteracy and indifference. One white informant said that only 15 to 20 Negroes in the entire county were educationally qualified to register. This same informant, however, stated that many unqualified white people were registered.

BAKER AND WEBSTER COUNTIES

In 1958, although Negroes constituted a majority of the population in both Baker and Webster, none was registered. As of the 1960 presidential elections, there were still none registered.

BLECKLEY, CHATTAHOOCHIE, FAYETTE, LINCOLN, MARION, MILLER, SEMINOLE, AND TREUTLEN COUNTIES

In 1959 the Commission reported that fewer than 3 percent of the voting-age Negroes in each of these counties were registered, although all had substantial Negro populations. Unfortunately, no current figures are available for any of these counties except Fayette, where, as of June 20, 1960, there were 26 Negroes (2.2 percent of the voting-age population) reported as registered.

At the time this report was prepared, the Department of Justice had inspected the voting records in four Georgia counties: Fayette, Webster, (mentioned above) Gwinnett, and Early. No suits to protect the right to vote had yet been filed in these counties.

Late in June of 1961, a group of Negroes filed suit in a Federal district court to enjoin the maintenance of segregated voting lists and polling places in Dougherty County, Ga.

Summary

The foregoing analysis shows that in at least 129 counties in 10 States, where Negroes constitute a substantial proportion of the population (more than 5 percent of the population 21 and over), less than 10 percent of those ostensibly eligible are in fact registered to vote. In 23 of these counties in 5 States, indeed, none at all are registered. Since similarly populated counties in each of the same States have large Negro registration, the inference is unavoidable that some affirmative deterrent is at work in those counties where none are registered. While not conclusive, this inference is sufficiently strong to warrant further specific inquiry in those "cipher" counties.

Another pattern that emerges is an inverse correlation between Negro concentration and Negro registration. Only in the border States of Delaware, Maryland, and West Virginia does this fail to appear. In the more Southern States, both on a statewide basis and in terms of counties, a greater concentration of Negroes generally means a smaller proportion of Negroes registered. Perhaps the reasons for this relationship is that the white community sees a high concentration of Negroes as a political threat and therefore feels impelled to prevent Negroes from voting. Certainly events in Macon County, Alabama, and Fayette and Haywood Counties, Tennessee, where the whites reacted vigorously to an apparent threat of Negro political inundation, suggests such a pattern. But other forces may also be at work: that is, a greater concentration of Negroes may often go hand-in-hand with a political, social, or economic structure in which factors other than discrimination tend to inhibit Negro voting. ....

THE OTHER DISFRANCHISED

The Constitution provides supposed immunity from voting restraints based on race or sex, but the states are otherwise free to fix qualifications on the right to vote as well as to regulate the conduct of elections, even for federal offices. Literacy, poll-tax, "good character," "good understanding," and other requirements, as well as intimidation, have effectively been used to disfranchise colored citizens. The immorality of the practice has long seared the national conscience. Yet many more Americans—white, middle-class Americans—are virtually disfranchised, without malice or prejudice, by unreasonably severe residency and registration requirements. This little understood phenomenon is discussed in the following selection from the testimony of Mr. Brendan Byrne, executive director of the American Heritage Foundation, before a recent Congressional investigating committee.

... $\mathscr{A}$T first we thought most nonvoters belonged to what we used to call the "Party of Indifference," but we have discovered there is another party—the "Party of Frustration." To this party belong more than 19 million good citizens who are prevented from voting through no fault of their own, but because of antiquated election laws.

Many of these laws were established 100 years ago and do not meet the needs of the highly mobile America of today.

Particularly, there is an interest in reducing residence requirements.

Subcommittee on Constitutional Amendments of the Senate Committee on the Judiciary, *Nomination and Election of President and Vice-President and Qualifications for Voting,* 87th Congress, 1st session, part II (Washington: G.P.O., 1961), pp. 467-478, *passim.*

We find from the U.S. Census Bureau that some 33 million people move every year. Many of these citizens lose their vote because they can't meet the residence requirements of their new State.

Senator KEFAUVER. You say your calculations show that 19 million people in the last election were not able to vote for the President, because of residence and difficulties of that kind?

Mr. BYRNE. Eight million of the 19 million were disenfranchised by residence requirements. Another 5 million were unable to vote—prevented because they were hospitalized and could not get absentee ballots. Nearly 3 million travelers were unable to vote because of inadequate absentee voting rules.

In my prepared statement there is a chart which breaks down the various other categories of disenfranchised voters. We hold no brief for people in prison and illiterates who cannot legally vote, but we do think that we should do something about outmoded residence requirements and other restrictions which keep millions of good citizens from the polls. . . .

(The statement submitted by Mr. Byrne follows:)

Penalizing Mobile Citizens

Archaic State residence requirements, many adopted a century ago, are the greatest single barrier to voting. An estimated 8 million voters out of 33 million people who moved last year were unable to vote in the 1960 elections because of inability to meet the State, or precinct residence requirements.

Twentieth century United States has a highly mobile population, but State residence laws have not kept pace with the mobility of our people. Despite the millions who move yearly, 35 States still require 1-year residence in the State; 3 demand 2 years; and 12 call for 6 months.

County and precinct residence requirements also present a problem. If you move to a new precinct in Milwaukee, Wis., you can reregister in 10 days. But in Natchez, Miss., you lose your right to vote for a year because Mississippi requires 1 year in the election district. In

Philadelphia and other cities, you can disfranchise yourself by moving across the street to a new district a month or two before election day. Confusion is compounded by the nationwide custom of observing September 30 as "moving day." ...

AMERICANS OF VOTING AGE UNABLE TO VOTE
IN THE NOVEMBER 1960 ELECTIONS

Total civilian population of voting age....................	107,000,000
Aliens of voting age......................................	3,000,000
Citizens of voting age.............................	104,000,000

Estimate of citizens of voting age unable to vote:

1. Mobile adults unable to meet State, county, or precinct residence requirements..........................	8,000,000
2. Adults kept from polls by illness at homes, hospitals, nursing homes, homes for aged, et cetera..........	5,000,000
3. Adults traveling for business, health, vacation and other reasons, unable to obtain absentee ballots..........	2,600,000
4. Adult Negroes in 11 Southern States kept from polls by rigged literacy tests, poll taxes, various social pressures, et cetera...............................	[1]1,750,000
5. Adult illiterates in 25 literacy-test States.............	800,000
6. Citizens of voting age in District of Columbia........	500,000
7. U.S. citizens living abroad........................	500,000
8. Adult prison population...........................	[2]215,000
9. Adult preachers of Jehovah Witnesses who face a religious disability to voting......................	225,000
Total citizens of voting age unable to vote............	19,590,000
Total citizens actually eligible to vote in 1960 elections..	84,410,000

[1] This is a modest estimate based on the findings of the Civil Rights Commission. The Congressional Quarterly puts poll tax and prejudice disfranchisement as high as 4,000,000. It is impossible to measure accurately the total number of voters kept from the polls by poll taxes, various social pressures on minority groups, and previous conviction of felony.
[2] Most States bar convicts, idiots, and the insane; others disfranchise paupers and vagrants. Mississippi bars tax-exempt Indians. Idaho denies the ballot to naturalized citizens of Mongolian descent. Florida disfranchises persons interested in an election wager. Rhode Island bars persons living on land ceded to the U. S. Government.
Sources: U. S. Census Bureau; American Heritage Foundation.

Total vote in 1960 presidential elections................ 68,832,818
Percentage of civilian voting populations which voted....   64.3
Percentage of citizens of voting age who voted..........   66.2
Percentage of actual eligibles who voted................   81.5

Disqualifying the Qualified

Who are these mobile victims of horse and buggy residence requirements? They include many of our better educated and more
responsible citizens—people with the initiative and character needed
to pull up stakes and seek advancement in a new community. Many
are educators, lawyers, clergymen; others are business executives.

A General Electric Co. spokesman reports that 6 percent of its
executive personnel were disfranchised in 1960 because of being
shifted from State to State.

A Newsweek editor confides, "I know a considerable number of
our own executives, salesmen, and editors who lost their 1960 vote
because of moving."

Oil companies, chainstores, and large corporations frequently
transfer engineers, managers, salesmen, and their executives. Each
change of residence within a year usually disfranchises two votes and
in some cases more. For example, eight executives of a New York
electronics firm were assigned to its Philadelphia branch last August
with the result that they and their wives could not cast their ballots
in November. . . .

Reduce Residence Requirements

Reduce State residence requirements for local, State, and congressional elections to 6 months and county requirements to 30 days.
These are the requirements in Idaho—national champion in getting
more of its citizens to the polls than any other State. A 1959 Gallup
survey shows that three out of four American adults approve the
adoption of uniform resident requirements for general elections with
6 months as the State maximum.

Protect the mobile voter by reducing State residence requirements for voting for President and Vice President as in Ohio, which requires 40 days residence; California, 54 days; or Missouri, 60 days. Or adopt a reciprocal arrangement similar to that of Wisconsin, Oregon, Connecticut, and Vermont. Wisconsin and Oregon allow a new resident to vote for President and Vice President if he can meet all other requirements and can show that he was a qualified voter in the State of his prior residence. Connecticut and Vermont allow a voter who moves permanently from the State to cast an absentee ballot for President and Vice President provided he files a declaration of intention to retain his voting residence for that purpose in his former State for a period of 24 months in Connecticut and 15 months in Vermont.

Permit voters moving within a State to vote in all elections in person or by absentee ballot in their former election district, should moving disqualify them from voting in the new district.

Modernize Absentee Voting

Besides residence requirements, another major bar to voting is the inadequate absentee balloting system in many States. The importance of absentee voting was dramatized in the 1960 presidential elections. California, counted safely in the Kennedy column the day after election, swung its vote to Nixon as a result of absentee ballots. Yet five States—New Mexico, Alabama, Louisiana, Mississippi and South Carolina still deny civilians the privilege of absentee voting by mail.

There is no valid reason why an otherwise qualified voter should forfeit his ballot because he is suddenly called out of town on business, or suffers a death in the family, or is incapacitated. Many States make no provision for balloting in such emergencies.

... An estimated 2.6 million travelers were prevented from voting in 1960 because of inadequate balloting laws. Another 5 million sick, hospitalized or disabled found it impossible in some States, or extremely difficult in others, to vote by absentee ballot. The same goes for an estimated 500,000 citizens living abroad.

The American public is overwhelmingly in favor of liberalizing absentee balloting. According to Dr. Gallup, 79 percent approve absentee ballots for travelers and 87 percent would make it easier for the ill, disabled, hospitalized and anyone else unable to get to the polls to vote by mail.

Absentee Voting Suggestions

Here are some suggestions for improving our absentee voting laws. Several have already been adopted or are under consideration by State legislatures.

Allow absentee voting by mail in both primary and general elections by all citizens of voting age away from their city or State on election day, as Michigan does. Safeguards against fraud should be maintained such as ballots of different colors for military and civilian voters, numbered ballots, careful checking of signatures, etc.

Extend absentee voting privileges to the hospitalized, sick, disabled and others unable to get to the polls, as Colorado and Nebraska have done.

Make it possible for all citizens of voting age outside of the United States to obtain absentee ballots sufficiently in advance so that the ballots may arrive at election boards before election day. All States extend this privilege to members of the Armed Forces. Why not civilians?

Allow citizens away from the country or State during registration periods, [for] example, 500,000 Americans abroad, to register by mail, as does Minnesota—with careful precautions and safeguards against fraud and heavy penalties for violations.

States requiring registration now permit members of the Armed Forces and their wives to register by mail. The same privilege should be accorded to civilians remotely situated from their home county.

Registration by mail is an essential part of absentee voting. Comparison of signatures and verification of mother's maiden name are a double guarantee against fraud in mail registration.

How Election Laws Affect Voting Turnout

States that make it easier to register and vote get more of their citizens to the polls.

In Idaho, voting champion among the 50 States, 80.7 percent of the voting population went to the polls in 1960. Idaho voters enjoy permanent tax-free registration and are allowed to register up to 3 days before the election. Only 6 months' residence in the State and 30 days in the county are required. There is no precinct residence requirement. It has a liberal absentee voting law and allows absentees to register by mail.

On the other hand, consider Mississippi, which had the poorest voting record in 1960—25.6 percent. Mississippi requires 2 years residence in the State and 1 year in the election district. It makes payment of a poll tax a condition for civilian voting and does not permit absentee balloting by civilians. No one may register after the first week in July. It also permits a literacy test requiring voters "to read, write and interpret reasonably any section of the State Constitution" —a subjective test that is not discrimination-proof.

Let's analyze the batting average of the States as compiled by the American Heritage Foundation:

Rank	State	Civilian population of voting age	Total vote	Percentage
1	Idaho	372,000	300,451	80.766
2	New Hampshire	367,000	295,761	80.588
3	Utah	469,000	374,981	79.953
4	North Dakota	350,000	278,431	79.551
5	South Dakota	388,000	306,087	78.831
6	West Virginia	1,085,000	837,781	77.214
7	Minnesota	2,003,000	1,541,887	76.978
8	Connecticut	1,590,000	1,222,883	76.910
9	Indiana	2,784,000	2,135,360	76.701

Rank	State	Civilian population of voting age	Total vote	Percentage
10	Massachusetts	3,230,000	2,469,480	76.454
11	Iowa	1,669,000	1,273,820	76.321
12	Illinois	6,244,000	4,757,394	76.191
13	Rhode Island	533,000	405,534	76.085
14	Wyoming	186,000	140,892	75.748
15	Delaware	264,000	196,683	74.501
16	Maine	574,000	421,767	73.478
17	Michigan	4,519,000	3,318,097	73.425
18	Alaska	83,000	60,762	73.207
19	Colorado	1,007,000	736,246	73.112
20	Missouri	2,651,000	1,934,422	72.969
21	Washington	1,703,000	1,241,572	72.905
22	Wisconsin	2,373,000	1,729,082	72.864
23	Vermont	230,000	167,324	72.749
24	New Jersey	3,827,000	2,773,111	72.461
25	Montana	387,000	277,579	71.725
26	Nebraska	857,000	613,095	71.530
27	Ohio	5,833,000	4,161,859	71.349
28	Oregon	1,089,000	775,462	71.208
29	Kansas	1,315,000	928,825	70.633
30	California	9,219,000	6,507,082	70.583
31	Pennsylvania	7,102,000	5,006,541	70.494
32	New York	10,788,000	7,291,079	67.584
33	Oklahoma	1,399,000	903,150	64.556
34	New Mexico	491,000	311,118	63.364
35	Nevada	174,000	107,267	61.647
36	Kentucky	1,876,000	1,124,462	59.939
37	Arizona	680,000	398,491	58.601
38	Maryland	1,819,000	1,055,349	58.017
39	Hawaii	321,000	184,745	57.552
40	North Carolina	2,521,000	1,368,966	54.302
41	Tennessee	2,079,000	1,051,792	50.591

Rank	State	Civilian population of voting age	Total vote	Percentage
42	Florida	3,099,000	1,544,180	49.828
43	Louisiana	1,770,000	807,891	45.604
44	Texas	5,329,000	2,311,670	43.379
45	Arkansas	1,029,000	428,509	41.643
46	Virginia	2,244,000	771,449	34.378
47	South Carolina	1,227,000	386,687	31.514
48	Georgia	2,342,000	733,349	31.312
49	Alabama	1,825,000	564,242	30.917
50	Mississippi	1,163,000	298,171	25.638

Source: The American Heritage Foundation; State Election Officials; U.S. Census Bureau.

The top eight States have laws that make it easier for all citizens to register and vote than the bottom eight.

The bottom eight include the five States (Alabama, Arkansas, Mississippi, Texas and Virginia) where no one can vote who hasn't paid the poll tax. Poll tax deadlines are generally months ahead of election day when interest in voting is lowest—Texas, January 31; Mississippi and Alabama, February 1; Virginia, May 7. Also in the bottom eight are three States that demand 2-year residence as a prerequisite of voting (Alabama, Mississippi and South Carolina); and four states that do not permit absentee civilians to vote by mail (Alabama, Louisiana, Mississippi and South Carolina). True, these States have a high illiteracy rate, but they also have the most formidable literacy tests.

Registration Reforms Needed

States ranking highest in turnout have superior registration and election administration systems. Here are some suggestions based on the experience of Ted Brown, Ohio's secretary of state, and other election officials.

Provide a uniform statewide system of permanent personal tax-free registration with central registration facilities open throughout the year. . . .

Conduct a general registration period with sufficient neighborhood registration centers ending, if possible, not sooner than 4 weeks before election day. A too early cutoff date discourages many citizens from qualifying. On the other hand, there must be an adequate interval before election days in larger cities to check the rolls for changes in residence, new registrants, deaths, etc. This would vary with the size of the city.

Set up mobile and special registration facilities in department stores, supermarkets and other public places—a practice effectually followed in Philadelphia, Los Angeles and Detroit. . . .

A Shorter Ballot

The greatest single barrier to informed voting is the long ballot. There is such a thing as asking voters to vote on so many issues and offices that they find it impossible to vote intelligently on any of them. A 1956 ballot in Little Rock, Ark., listed 169 elective offices to be filled by the voters.

Donald M. Nicholson, Denver election official, reports that in 1960, Denver voters were expected to make intelligent and well-informed decisions on 7 constitutional issues and 95 candidates for 45 offices.

The Oregon ballot is so long and confusing that school textbooks cite it as the worst ballot in the United States, admits Jack F. Thompson, State director of elections.

Voting participation would soar if voters were not confronted with a bewilderingly long ballot of local, State and National candidates, says former U. S. Senator Edward J. Thye, of Minnesota.

President Woodrow Wilson once confessed his ignorance of 80 percent of the candidates he voted for. In 1959 nearly 9 out of 10 voters stated that they knew little or nothing about candidates listed on the ballot, according to Dr. Gallup.

How short should the ballot be? It should be short enough to enable the voter to make decisions on an informed basis. Richard S. Childs, founder of the short ballot movement, believes it should contain no more than five choices.

The logical way to shorten the ballot is to remove all minor non-policy-making offices as coroner, sheriff, etc.; and all important offices of a specialized character on which the voter is not qualified to judge; for example, judges, treasurer, attorney general, etc.

The average voter is no more equipped to choose judges, comptrollers, secretaries of States, engineers, and a host of other offices still on many State and local ballots than he is to select the head of the Atomic Energy Commission or Federal Reserve System. A better method would be to remove such technical posts from the ballot and appoint them on the basis of civil service examinations or some other kind of merit system. According to Dr. Gallup, the majority of American adults (52 percent) favor such a move.

Besides stimulating more thoughtful voting, a shorter ballot would help reduce the number of voters who sometimes fail to vote because of confusion over the long list of candidates and issues. A 1959 Gallup study showed that nearly one voter in five admitted occasionally failing to vote because of the long ballot and uncertainty about the mechanics of voting.

Gobbledygook

Another barrier to voting is the bombastic and long-winded language describing constitutional amendments, propositions, and referendums. "The surest way to kill a referendum is to frame it in jargon no voter can understand," says Robert C. Zimmerman, Wisconsin secretary of state.

One result of ballot bombast is that many voters are so confused that they refrain from voting. For example, in the 1960 elections 513,511 Wisconsin voters who voted for President failed to express a choice on an important State referendum.

A few years ago, President Eisenhower, emerging from his Gettysburg polling place, complained that he had trouble unraveling the pompous prose of several constitutional amendments on the Pennsylvania ballot.

Recently, the voters of Englewood, N.J., were confronted with this ballot puzzle: "Shall the provision to substitute No. 3 of title No. 11 under the revised statutes of New Jersey as amended and supplemented, relating to civil service, be adopted in the city of Englewood, county of Bergen, State of New Jersey?" Translation: Should Englewood's city employees be placed in civil service status?

The remedy is obvious—simple English as in a recent New Hampshire ballot. Instead of mystifying the electorate, the ballot plainly asked: "Are you in favor of permitting absentee voting in primary elections?" California's amendments are also clearly stated in layman's language. . . .

Other Suggestions

Literacy tests should be prepared by educators and should be objective and discrimination-proof. Such a test is New York's which consists of reading a short paragraph and answering eight simple questions of fact.

Hold primary elections in late May or early June. Late June, July, and August are poor because of vacations. Most election officials oppose September primaries because of insufficient time for absentee balloting, handling recounts, etc.

If feasible, remove residence and absentee voting requirements from State constitutions. The difficulty of amending these constitutions is a serious obstacle to modernizing election laws. Many States require approval of two consecutive legislative sessions and popular referendum. Amending some State constitutions requires constitutional conventions, some of which meet only every 10 or 20 years. Also some State legislatures do not meet every year. . . .

ARE SOME VOTES MORE EQUAL

THAN OTHERS

One of the scandals of American political life is the inequitable apportionment of representation in the legislatures of the land. In Vermont, for example, where the House of Representatives has not been redistricted since 1793, one town with thirty-eight people has the same representation in the House as another with a population of 33,000. A majority of the California Senate can be elected by 10.7% of the population; one rural district with a population of 14,294 elects the same number of Senators as Los Angeles County with a population over six million. Only six states have so apportioned seats that 40% or more of the population is required to elect a majority of the legislators in both houses. Urban and suburban voters are generally at the mercy of conservative rural voters. Until 1962 no remedy for this situation could be had in the federal courts on the theory that the issue was "political" or "nonjusticiable." Then the Supreme Court suddenly switched its position, and a rash of suits in nearly thirty states was swiftly begun. In one of the first and most significant cases heralding reform, the Georgia County Unit system was declared unconstitutional by the United States Court of Appeals, Fifth Circuit.

Before TUTTLE and BELL, Circuit Judges, and
HOOPER, District Judge
GRIFFIN B. BELL, Circuit Judge

PLAINTIFF seeks declaratory and injunctive relief alleging deprivation of federal constitutional rights. The prayer seeks to restrain

Sanders *v.* Gray, 203 F. Supp. 158 (April 28, 1962).

the Georgia State Democratic Party and the Chairman and Secretary of the Georgia State Democratic Executive Committee in their representative capacities, and their successors in office, from conducting elections under the County Unit System; from tabulating and consolidating ballots cast in the Democratic primary election to be held on September 12, 1962, and in any other primary election conducted by that party on the basis of the County Unit System; from selecting any nominee on the basis of ballots cast in any primary election held on the County Unit System; . . . and from giving force and effect to the County Unit System as it is established under the Neill Primary Act. . . . Lastly, plaintiff seeks judgment to the effect that the Neill Primary Act is void and unconstitutional insofar as it provides for the nomination by the defendant party of any candidates for the named offices under the County Unit System.

Plaintiff is an elector within the meaning of Article II, § I, Paragraphs I through IV of the Constitution of the State of Georgia of 1945, Ga.Code §§ 2-701 through 2-704. He is qualified to vote in primary and general elections in Fulton County, is a member of the Democratic Party of Georgia, intends to vote in the Democratic primary election to be held within the State of Georgia in 1962 and intends to support the nominees of such primary in the general election to be held on the Tuesday after the first Monday in November, 1962. . . .

Plaintiff contends in his suit that the County Unit System is arbitrary and discriminatory to the extent that it is a denial to him of equal protection of the laws within the meaning of the Fourteenth Amendment to the Federal Constitution in that Fulton County where he resides, the largest county in Georgia, is allotted only six unit votes under the statute which in total allows six unit votes each for the eight largest counties by population in Georgia, four unit votes for each of the thirty next largest by population and two each for the remaining one hundred twenty one counties. According to the 1960 United States census Fulton County had a population of 556,326 while Georgia had a total population according to the same source of 3,-943,116, Fulton County thus having 14.11 percent of the total population of Georgia but only 1.46 percent of the total of 410 county unit votes. On the other hand, the least populous county in Georgia, Echols, had a population according to the 1960 census of 1876 or .05 percent of the population in the state, and is accorded two units or .48 percent of the total units. Thus the discrimination runs against Fulton County on an approximate ten to one ratio based on population and in favor of Echols County on an approximate ten to one ratio. The discriminatory ratio under the County Unit System runs, based on the 1960 census, between these ranges but in every instance against Fulton County. The Unit System also accords to the candidate receiving the plurality of votes in a county the entire unit vote thus reversing the votes of those voting for another candidate just as is the case under the Federal Electoral College System.

Plaintiff asserts, in addition to his Fourteenth Amendment claim, that the System violates the Seventeenth Amendment which provides that the Senators from each state shall be elected by the people thereof. . . .

HISTORY OF THE COUNTY UNIT SYSTEM

The County Unit System throughout its long use in primary elections in Georgia, first by party rule and later by statute, has always been based on the formula obtaining for apportionment of the [Ga.] House of Representatives. . . .

Under the Unit System candidates for governor and United States senator are required to receive a majority of the votes cast to secure the respective nominations out of the total of 410 county unit votes (two for each member of the House of Representatives). In the event of a tie the candidate with the largest popular vote becomes the nominee. A second or run off primary is held if no candidate has the majority. A plurality is sufficient as to the other offices to which the County Unit System applies. . . .

PREVIOUS LITIGATION CONCERNING
THE COUNTY UNIT SYSTEM

The validity of the County Unit System was first challenged in the case of Cook v. Fortson, N.D.Ga., 1946, 68 F. Supp. 624, where an effort was made to have the county unit rule and the statutes permitting its use declared unconstitutional, and to enjoin its use in determining the Democratic nominee for Congress for the Fifth District of Georgia. The winner received a majority of the county unit vote but another candidate received a majority of the popular vote. Injunctive relief was denied on the basis of Colegrove v. Greene, 1946, 328 U.S. 549, 66 S.Ct. 1198, 90 L.Ed. 1432, leaving the inequality complained of for consideration by the State Legislature or by the Congress under Article I, § 4 of the Federal Constitution. . . .

Another suit was instituted in 1950, this time prior to the primary, challenging the unit system and it was dismissed by the District Court. South v. Peters, 89 F.Supp. 672 (N.D.Ga., 1950), Judge Andrews dissenting. The Supreme Court affirmed per curiam, 339 U.S. 276, 70 S. Ct. 641, 94 L.Ed. 834, saying, "Federal courts consistently refuse to exercise their equity powers in cases posing political issues arising from a state's geographical distribution of electoral strength among its political subdivisions," citing MacDougall v. Green, 1948, 335 U.S. 281, 69 S.Ct. 1, 93 L.Ed. 3; Colegrove, supra; Wood v. Broom, 1932, 287 U.S. 1, 53 S.Ct. 1, 77 L.Ed. 131; and Johnson v. Stevenson, 5 Cir., 1948, 170 F.2d 108. South v. Peters, 1950, 339 U.S. 276, 70 S.Ct. 641, 94 L.Ed. 834. Justices Douglas and Black dissented. . . . They set out their view of what the rule should be and it turned out to be the forerunner of things to come, Baker v. Carr, 82 S.Ct. 691. It was that "the only tenable premise under the Fourteenth, Fifteenth, and Seventeenth Amendments is that where nominations are made in primary elections, there shall be no inequality in voting power by reason of race, creed, color or other invidious discrimination." . . .

JURISDICTION, JUSTICIABILITY, STANDING
AND THE QUESTION PRESENTED

A calm in litigation ensued thereafter as to the County Unit System while so-called reapportionment litigation was taking place in other states and some at least was pending before the Supreme Court. Baker v. Carr, supra. The instant litigation was filed shortly after the announcement of the decision in that case, and on the same day. A three-judge court was duly constituted and the matter came on promptly for hearing on the application for interlocutory injunction.

That case involved the apportionment of the Tennessee State Legislature. The court held that the District Court possessed jurisdiction of the subject matter, and that a justiciable cause of action was stated upon which the appellants, residents and voters of Tennessee claiming arbitrary and capricious state action offensive to the Fourteenth Amendment, had standing to maintain the suit. The rationale of that decision encompasses the cause of action here. We, accordingly, take jurisdiction and also hold that plaintiff has standing to maintain the suit and that the complaint sets out a justiciable issue.

In doing so, we, of course, resolve in favor of the plaintiff the question whether the Fourteenth Amendment protection extends to alleged deprivation of equal protection occurring in a Primary, as distinguished from a General election.

Much has been said in briefs and oral argument as to the place which the Primary in the State of Georgia has traditionally played in the election process. It is a fact known to all that the Democratic candidate has, without exception, at least during the present century, been the choice of the voters at the General election. On the other hand, it is pointed out that at least with respect to the office of Governor, a candidate has been nominated by the Republican party to participate in the General election in November of this year. Our conclusion that the protection of the Fourteenth Amendment extends to invidious discriminations if they exist in a party primary in Georgia in no way depends upon the degree to which the Democratic party primary is tantamount to the final election. It is based rather on prior decisions of the Court of Appeals for the Fifth Circuit, where it has been held that the conduct of a Primary election in Georgia is such an essential part in the total election process, its conduct and management is so closely supervised by State law and the effect to be given it is so clearly determined by statute that the action of the party in the conduct of its primary constitutes state action within the contemplation of the Fourteenth Amendment to the Constitution (Chapman v. King, 5 Cir., 154 F.2d 460). . . .

The remaining questions presented are but two: Does the County Unit System as set out in the Neill Primary Act, amended, violate the right of plaintiff to equal protection of the laws under the Fourteenth Amendment or his right to vote for a United States senator under the Seventeenth Amendment. This latter right would reach the unit system only as to the primary election for the office of United States senator, while the former would reach it as to all state-wide offices. A subsidiary question of prime, even overriding importance, is the test to be applied to determine violation, and the factors to be considered in making the test.

THE TEST TO BE APPLIED

. . . We do not doubt that the Fourteenth Amendment applies, and we proceed on that basis. We think the Court by its opinion in Baker v. Carr has now adopted the following test stated by Mr. Justice Douglas in South v. Peters, supra:

"Where nominations are made in primary elections, there shall be no inequality in voting power by reason of race, creed, color or other invidious discrimination."

Having applied the equal protection clause of the Fourteenth Amendment to the rights of plaintiff in this suit, and having set aside for the purpose of this hearing and decision the other points raised by all parties, we apply the test of invidious discrimination. We need not apply it of course to the "time honored" system but to the system which is new as of yesterday. And as a part of the application of the test we hold that a political party may use a county unit system in primary elections for the nomination of candidates in the general election if the system, as we shall point out, does not run afoul of constitutional inhibitions.

A test for invidiousness must be formulated. Unlike per se invidiousness, springing from discrimination based on race, creed or color, we must here deal with discrimination not so infected, but arising out of a state legislative classification diffusing party political strength. The diffusion is between counties of all sizes, sparsely to densely populated, apparently on a rural-urban basis, but weighted from top to bottom, county by county, in favor of the next smaller.

We make the test on a consideration of all relevant factors, and these include rationality of state policy. See the concurring opinion of Mr. Justice Clark in Baker v. Carr where the dismissal of the appeal in South v. Peters, supra, was said to reflect the viewpoint of the Supreme Court "to refrain from intervening where there is some rational policy behind the State's system."

Another test is whether or not the system is arbitrary. The right of plaintiff in this connection depends upon the treatment accorded his unit. His unit, Fulton County, must be related to the state as a whole in measuring his right, and his right is the same as that of all other Democrats in his unit. The fact that Echols or some other small county receives more than its share is of no concern to Fulton County so long as it is accorded proper treatment. And the consideration of this factor includes the applicability of the diffusion principle—the right of a state to properly diffuse "political initiative as between its thinly populated counties and those having concentrated masses, in view of the fact that the latter have practical opportunities for exerting their political weight at the polls not available to the former. The Constitution—a practical instrument of government—makes no such demands on the States." MacDougall v. Green, supra, 335 U.S. at page 284, 69 S.Ct. at page 2, 93 L.Ed. 3. We have considered too the genesis of the System, whether or not it was for a fair purpose in the beginning—that it was is self-evident from the history heretofore set out.

Another important factor to be considered in making the test is whether or not the unit system has a historical basis in our political institutions, both federal and state. The primary in Georgia and elsewhere simply took the place of the convention. The county units took the place of county delegates. Counties were governmental units in Georgia before the Union and had their voice in the councils of government on the state level through representation, rationally apportioned, first on number of electors and later on population, but never in any exact proportion. And for many years governors were elected by these representatives. With the advent of popular elections of the governor and other state officials, conventions with delegate strength by party rule based on county apportionment in the House of Representatives became the medium of nomination. Delegates were elected, not by direct primary, but at county mass meetings. This was followed by the county primary for the election of delegates—still in the ratio of legislative apportionment, and later by statewide primaries but still by party rule. And this finally became the statutory mode—as in the statute under attack here. . . .

Another important consideration in making the test, at least for the purpose of court intervention, is the presence or absence of political remedy. This lack is implicit in Baker v. Carr. Here we are not dealing with legislative apportionment but with the management of the state Democratic Party. Plaintiff as a Democrat is complaining of treatment received by him at the hand of other Democrats through the medium of a state statute, sponsored by a governor from his party and enacted by a legislature consisting in the main of members of his party. A political remedy encompasses the give and take within the political arena, but we must consider it, and whether there is substantial likelihood under the existing system of plaintiff's obtaining such relief measures as may be needed to accord him his constitutional rights. We hold that there is not.

An additional factor of importance, and of which we are much aware is the delicate relationship between the federal and state governments under the Constitution. It has long been the law that the violation in question must be clear before a federal court of equity will [lend] its power to the disruption of the state election processes.

The test is on the sum of all of these factors, and if the action—here the statute, complained of—offends what are thought to be fundamental political concepts, giving due regard to each factor and to the rights of plaintiff and all others in his suit as compared to the whole—the state, it must be stricken because of discrimination so excessive as to be invidious.

THE MERITS

The system as it existed prior to yesterday was violative of the right of plaintiff to equal protection of the laws. The system as it exists today is an improvement, and is the result of an effort on the part of the responsible state officials and the General Assembly of Georgia within recent days to comport with sharp new legal precedents. But even the new system misses the mark in two respects: first in failing to accord the unit of plaintiff a reasonable proportion of the whole, and second in failing to accord the units representing a majority of the population a reasonable proportion of the whole. We do not strike the county unit system as such. We do strike it in its present form.[1]

[1] The following table will illustrate how under the recent statute the vote of each citizen counts for less and less as the population of the county of his residence increases, this table covering only the four largest and four smallest counties in comparison with Fulton, the largest:

County Number	Name	Population	Number Unit Votes	Population per unit vote	Ratio to Fulton County
1	Fulton	556,326	40	13,908	
2	DeKalb	256,782	20	12,839	
3	Chatham	188,299	16	11,760	
4	Muscogee	158,623	14	11,330	
156	Webster	3,247	2	1,623	8 to 1
157	Glascock	2,672	2	1,336	10 to 1
158	Quitman	2,432	2	1,216	11 to 1
159	Echols	1,876	2	938	14 to 1

There are 97 two-unit counties, totalling 194 unit votes, and 22 counties totalling 66 unit votes, altogether 260 unit votes, within 14 of a majority; but no county in the

And while it may appear doctrinaire to some extent in the application of such broad constitutional rights as equal protection, Mac-Dougall, supra, to state definite standards, we nevertheless, because, and only because, it is a question of much public moment, hold that a unit system for use in a party primary is invidiously discriminatory if any unit has less than its share to the nearest whole number proportionate to population, or to the whole of the vote in a recent party gubernatorial primary, or to the whole vote for electors of the party in a recent presidential election; provided no discrimination is deemed to be invidious under the system if the disparity against any county is not in excess of the disparity that exists against any state in the most recent electoral college allocation, or under the equal proportions formula for representation of the several states in the Congress, and provided it is adjusted to accord with changes in the basis at least once each ten years. This is a "judicially manageable standard" contemplated in Baker v. Carr, supra.

Due consideration has been given to delaying the entry of an injunction until the next regular session of the General Assembly in January but having recognized the constitutional right of plaintiff, we cannot fail to protect it, nor do we believe the state would want to deny it in the fall primary.

An interlocutory injunction will be entered enjoining and restraining defendants from giving application to the County Unit System by statute or party rule in any election where the allocation of units falls short of this standard.

---

above has as much as 20,000 population. The remaining 40 counties range in population from 20,481 to 556,326, but they control altogether only 287 county unit votes. Combination of the units from the counties having the smallest population gives counties having population of one-third of the total in the state a clear majority of county units.

III.   The Powers of the President

THE NATURE OF THE PRESIDENCY

A President's conception of the office of the Presidency and of himself as the leader of his party very largely influences his effectiveness as President, regardless of his policy views. With some oversimplification, historians tend to classify Presidents as "strong" or "weak." Theodore Roosevelt spoke for the former class when he reminisced, "My belief was that it was not only his [the President's] right but his duty to do anything that the needs of the Nation demanded unless such action was forbidden by the Constitution or by the law." His successor, William Howard Taft, took the opposing view "that a President can exercise no power which cannot fairly and reasonably be traced to some specific grant of power. . . ." The modern view of the Presidency—and surely the view of the present incumbent—has been ably summed up by former President Harry S. Truman in the following selection from an address delivered in 1954.

. . . *W*HEN the founding fathers outlined the Presidency in Article II of the Constitution, they left a great many details out and vague. I think they relied on the experience of the nation to fill in the outlines. The office of chief executive has grown with the progress of this great republic. It has responded to the many demands that our complex society has made upon the Government. It has given our nation a means of meeting our greatest emergencies. Today, it is one of the most important factors in our leadership of the free world.

Many diverse elements entered into the creation of the office,

Harry S. Truman, Speech delivered at the Truman Birthday Party, New York, N. Y., May 8, 1954, reported in the *New York Times*, May 9, 1954, p. 54.

springing, as it did, from the parent idea of the separation of powers.

There was the firm conviction of such powerful and shrewd minds as that of John Adams that the greatest protection against unlimited power lay in an executive secured against the encroachment of the national assembly. Then there were the fears of those who suspected a plot to establish a monarchy on these shores. Others believed that the experience under the Confederation showed above all the need of stability through a strong central administration. Finally, there was the need for compromise among these and many other views.

The result was a compromise—a compromise which that shrewd observer, Alexis de Tocqueville, over 120 years ago, believed would not work. He thought that the Presidential office was too weak. The President, he thought, was at the mercy of Congress. The President could recommend, to be sure, he thought, but the President had no power and the Congress had the power. The Congress could disregard his recommendations, overrule his vetoes, reject his nominations. De Tocqueville thought that no man of parts, worthy of leadership, would accept so feeble a role.

This was not a foolish view and there was much in our early history which tended to bear it out. But there is a power in the course of events which plays its own part. In this case again, Justice Holmes' epigram proved true. He said a page of history is worth a volume of logic. And as the pages of history were written they unfolded powers in the Presidency not explicitly found in Article II of the Constitution.

In the first place, the President became the leader of a political party. The party under his leadership had to be dominant enough to put him in office. This political party leadership was the last thing the Constitution contemplated. The President's election was not intended to be mixed up in the hurly-burly of partisan politics. . . . The people were to choose wise and respected men who would meet in calm seclusion and choose a President and the runner-up would be Vice President.

All of this went by the board—though most of the original language remains in the Constitution. Out of the struggle and tumult of the political arena a new and different President emerged—the man who led a political party to victory and retained in his hands the power of party leadership. That is, he retained it like the sword Excalibur, if he could wrest it from the scabbard and wield it.

Another development was connected with the first. As the President came to be elected by the whole people, he became responsible to the whole people. I used to say the only lobbyist the whole people had in Washington was the President of the United States. Our whole people looked to him for leadership, and not confined within the limits of a written document. Every hope and every fear of his fellow citizens, almost every aspect of their welfare and activity, falls within the scope of his concern—indeed, it falls within the scope of his duty. Only one who has held that office can really appreciate that. It is the President's responsibility to look at all questions from the point of view of the whole people. His written and spoken word commands national and often international attention.

These powers which are not explicitly written into the Constitution are powers which no President can pass on to his successor. They go only to him who can take and use them. However, it is these powers, quite as much as those enumerated in Article II of the Constitution which make the Presidential system unique and which give the papers of Presidents their peculiar and revealing importance.

For it is through the use of these great powers that leadership arises, events are molded and administrations take on their character. Their use can make a Jefferson or a Lincoln Administration; their non-use can make a Buchanan or a Grant Administration.

Moreover, a study of these aspects of our governmental and political history will save us from self-righteousness—from taking a holier than thou attitude toward other nations. For brilliant and enduring as were the minds of the architects of our Constitution, they did not devise a foolproof system to protect us against the disaster of a weak government—that is, government unable to face and resolve—one way or another—pressing national problems. Indeed, in some respects, the separation of powers requires stronger executive leadership than does the parliamentary and cabinet system.

As Justice Brandeis used to say, the separation of powers was not devised to promote efficiency in government. In fact, it was devised to prevent one form of deficiency—absolutism or dictatorship. By making the Congress separate and independent in the exercise of its powers, and the executive separate and independent in the exercise of its powers, a certain amount of political conflict was built into the Constitution. For the price of independence is eternal vigilance and a good deal of struggle. And this is not a bad thing—on the contrary, it is a good thing for the preservation of the liberty of the people—if it does not become conflict just for its own sake.

I've always said that the President who didn't have a fight with the Congress wasn't any good anyhow. And that is no reflection on the Congress. They are always looking after their rights. You needn't doubt that.

Having been in these two branches of government, legislative and executive, I think I am expressing a considered and impartial opinion in saying that the powers of the President are much more difficult to exercise and to preserve from encroachment than those of the Congress. In part, this comes from the difficulty of the problems of our time, and from the fact that upon the President falls the responsibility of obtaining action, timely and adequate to meet the nation's needs. Whatever the Constitution says, he is held responsible for any disaster which may come.

And so a successful administration is one of strong Presidential leadership. Weak leadership—or no leadership—produces failure and often disaster.

This does not come from the inherent incapacity of the people of the nation. It is inherent in legislative government where there is no executive strong and stable enough to rally the people to a sustained effort of will and prepared to use its power of party control to the fullest extent.

Today, also, one of the great responsibilities and opportunities of the President is to lead and inspire public opinion. The words of a President carry great weight. His acts carry even more weight.

All of us remember the words of Franklin D. Roosevelt in his first inaugural address which did so much to rally the spirit of a nation struggling through the depths of a depression. He said, "The only thing we have to fear is fear itself." These words, however, would have had little effect if President Roosevelt had not backed them up by action. Following that speech, President Roosevelt plunged into a vigorous course, striking at the depression on all fronts. He backed his words by his action, and words and action restored the faith of the nation in its government and in its form of government, too.

Today, there is the same need for a similar combination of words and action concerning the hysteria about communism. Our country has acted firmly and resolutely to hold Communist imperialism in check. Nevertheless, that concern has created fear and fear has been played upon by persons who see in it an easy way to influence votes. There is no dispute any more that this unreasonable fear exists. The leaders of both political parties have acknowledged it. . . . We all know the corrosive effect of this hysteria and the dangers it holds.

But, as I have said, the office of the Presidency is the one office of our Government to which all the people turn when they are beset by fears like these. It is to the President that they look to say a firm "No" to those who wish to destroy others through fear and innuendo. It is his duty to defend the unjustly accused and demonstrate in the executive branch of the Government that the ancient principles of fair play and decency prevail all the time. By such deeds and acts the Presidency can reassure the nation and stem the growth of hysteria.

Again, we see today history repeating itself as the legislative branch of the Government, under the overshadowing fear of communism, expands its functions and activities into the very center of the power of the executive branch.

The President is responsible for the administration of his office. And that means for the administration of the entire executive branch. It is not the business of Congress to run the agencies of government for the President.

Unless this principle is observed, it is impossible to have orderly government. The legislative power will ooze into the executive offices. It will influence and corrupt the decisions of the executive branch. It will affect promotions and transfers. It will warp and twist policies.

Not only does the President cease to be master in his own house, but the whole house of government becomes one which has no master. The power of decision then rests only in the legislative branch, and the legislative branch by its very nature is not equipped to perform these executive functions.

To this kind of encroachment it is the duty of the President to say firmly and flatly, "No, you can't do it." The investigative power of Congress is not limitless. It extends only so far as to permit the Congress to acquire the information that it honestly needs to exercise its legislative functions. Exercised beyond those limits, it becomes a manifestation of unconstitutional power. It raises the threat of legislative dictatorship and that's the worst dictatorship in the world.

Our nation was once almost torn apart by such an expansion of Congressional power. That was in the age of President Johnson, when the Radical Republicans of that time tried to take over the functions of the President. But we cannot afford such an attack on the Presidency by today's version of the Radical Republicans.

Today the perils and problems which threaten us and our allies make all the difficulties of the Reconstruction period—that tragic era —seem rather pale. Today the tasks of leadership falling upon the President spring not only from our national problems but from those of the whole world. Today that leadership will determine whether our Government will function effectively, and upon its functioning depends the survival of each of us and also on that depends the survival of the free world, if I may be so bold as to say that.

And today our Government cannot function properly unless it follows the provisions of the Constitution. Our Government cannot function properly unless the President is master in his own house and unless the executive departments and agencies of the Government, including the armed forces, are responsible to the President. . . .

PRESIDENTIAL INFLUENCE

During World War II, President Roosevelt, provoked by Congressional procrastination in enacting price controls, warned: "In the event that Congress should fail to act, and act adequately, I shall accept the responsibility, and I will act. . . . When the war is won, the powers under which I act automatically revert to the people—to whom they belong." The war powers of the President are practically unlimited, but in peacetime his real authority is largely the product of his political effectiveness. Presidential "power" was never more extraordinarily demonstrated than when President Kennedy angrily criticized the United States Steel Corporation for its inflationary price increases. Within a few days the giant company and its emulators capitulated by canceling the increases. That Kennedy did not rely only on his rhetorical gifts and his influence upon public opinion is evident from the attack upon his "police state" methods by the joint Senate-House Republican leadership. Here is the President's sensational press conference statement, followed by the partisan criticism of the opposition party.

Kennedy Assaults U.S. Steel

THE PRESIDENT: I have several announcements to make.

Steel Price Increase

Simultaneous and identical actions of United States Steel and other leading steel corporations increasing steel prices by some $6 a ton

Transcript of President Kennedy's Press Conference, April 11, 1962, and the "G.O.P. Statement on Steel," from the *New York Times*, April 12 and April 20, 1962.

constitute a wholly unjustifiable and irresponsible defiance of the public interest.

In this serious hour in our Nation's history, when we are confronted with grave crises in Berlin and Southeast Asia, when we are devoting our energies to economic recovery and stability, when we are asking reservists to leave their homes and families for months on end and servicemen to risk their lives—and four were killed in the last two days in Vietnam—and asking union members to hold down their wage increases, at a time when restraint and sacrifice are being asked of every citizen, the American people will find it hard, as I do, to accept a situation in which a tiny handful of steel executives whose pursuit of private power and profit exceeds their sense of public responsibility can show such utter contempt for the interests of 185 million Americans.

If this rise in the cost of steel is imitated by the rest of the industry, instead of rescinded, it would increase the cost of homes, autos, appliances, and most other items for every American family. It would increase the cost of machinery and tools to every American businessman and farmer. It would seriously handicap our efforts to prevent an inflationary spiral from eating up the pensions of our older citizens, and our new gains in purchasing power.

It would add, Secretary McNamara informed me this morning, an estimated $1 billion to the cost of our defenses, at a time when every dollar is needed for national security and other purposes. It would make it more difficult for American goods to compete in foreign markets, more difficult to withstand competition from foreign imports, and thus more difficult to improve our balance of payments position, and stem the flow of gold. And it is necessary to stem it for our national security, if we are going to pay for our security commitments abroad. And it would surely handicap our efforts to induce other industries and unions to adopt responsible price and wage policies.

The facts of the matter are that there is no justification for an increase in the steel prices. The recent settlement between the industry and the union, which does not even take place until July 1st, was widely acknowledged to be non-inflationary, and the whole purpose and effect of this Administration's role, which both parties understood, was to achieve an agreement which would make unnecessary any increase in prices. Steel output per man is rising so fast that labor costs per ton of steel can actually be expected to decline in the next 12 months. And in fact, the Acting Commissioner of the Bureau of Labor Statistics informed me this morning that, and I quote: "Employment costs per unit of steel output in 1961 were essentially the same as they were in 1958."

The cost of the major raw materials, steel scrap and coal, has also been declining, and for an industry which has been generally operating at less than two-thirds of capacity, its profit rate has been normal and can be expected to rise sharply this year in view of the reduction in idle capacity.

Their lot has been easier than that of 100,000 steel workers thrown out of work in the last three years. The industry's cash dividends have exceeded $600 million in each of the last five years, and earnings in the first quarter of this year were estimated in the February 28th Wall Street Journal to be among the highest in the history.

In short, at a time when they could be exploring how more efficient and better prices could be obtained reducing prices in this industry in recognition of lower costs, their unusually good labor contract, their foreign competition and their increase in production and profits which are coming this year, a few gigantic corporations have decided to increase prices in ruthless disregard of their public responsibilities.

The Steel Workers Union can be proud that it abided by its responsibilities in this agreement. And this government also has responsibilities which we intend to meet. The Department of Justice and the Federal Trade Commission are examining the significance of this action in a free, competitive economy. The Department of Defense and other agencies are reviewing its impact on their policies of procurement and I am informed that steps are underway by those members of the Congress who plan appropriate inquiries into how these price decisions are so quickly made and reached, and what legislative safeguards may be needed to protect the public interest.

Price and wage decisions in this country, except for . . . very limited restrictions in the case of monopolies and national emergency strikes, are and ought to be freely and privately made, but the American people have a right to expect in return for that freedom, a higher sense of business responsibility for the welfare of their country than has been shown in the last two days.

Some time ago I asked each American to consider what he would do for his country. And I asked the steel companies. In the last 24 hours we had their answer. . . .

Q. Mr. President, the unusually strong language which you used in discussing the steel situation would indicate that you might be considering some pretty strong action. Are you thinking in terms of requesting or reviving the need for wage-price controls?

THE PRESIDENT: I think that my statement states what the situation is today. This is a free country. In all the conversations which were held by members of this Administration and myself with the leaders of the steel union and the companies, it was always very obvious that they could proceed with freedom to do what they thought was best within the limitations of law. But I did very clearly emphasize on every occasion that my only interest was that in trying to secure an agreement which would not provide an increase in prices, because I thought that price stability in steel would have the most far-reaching consequences for industrial and economic stability and for our position abroad, and price instability would have the most far-reaching consequences in making our lot much more difficult.

When the agreement was signed—and the agreement was a moderate one and within the range of productivity increases, as I have said—actually, there will be reduction in cost per unit during the next year—I thought, I was hopeful, we had achieved our goal. Now the actions that will be taken will be—are being now considered by the Administration. The Department of Justice is, particularly in view of the very speedy action of the companies who have entirely different economic problems facing them than did United States Steel, the speed with which they moved, it seems to me to require an examination of our present laws, and whether they are being obeyed, by the Federal Trade Commission, and by the Department of Justice. I am very interested in the respective investigations that will be conducted in the House and Senate, and whether we shall need additional legislation, which I would come to very reluctantly. But I must say the last 24 hours indicates that those with great power are not always concerned about the national interest.

Q. In your conversation with Mr. Blough [President of U.S. Steel Corp.] yesterday, did you make a direct request that this price increase be either deferred or rescinded?

THE PRESIDENT: I was informed about the price increase after the announcement had gone out to the papers. I told Mr. Blough of my very keen disappointment and what I thought would be the most unfortunate effects of it. And of course we were hopeful that other companies who I have said, have a different situation in regard to profits and all of the rest than U.S. Steel. They all have somewhat different economic situations. I was hopeful particularly in view of the statement in the paper by the President of Bethlehem in which he stated—although now he says he is misquoted—that there should be no price increase and we are investigating that statement. I was hopeful that the others would not follow the example and therefore the pressures of the competitive marketplace would bring United States Steel back to their original prices. But the parade began. But it came to me after the decision was made, there was no prior consultation or information given to me. . . .

Q. Mr. President, if I could get back to steel for a minute, you mentioned an investigation into the suddenness of the decision to increase prices. Did you—is it the position of the Administration that it believed it had the assurance of the steel industry at the time of the recent labor agreement that it would not increase prices? Is that a breach of their . . .

THE PRESIDENT: We did not ask either side to give us any assurance, because there is a very proper limitation to the power of the Government in this free economy. All we did in our meetings was to emphasize how important it was that there be price stability, and we stressed that our whole purpose in attempting to persuade the union to begin to bargain early and to make an agreement which would not affect prices, of course, was for the purpose of maintaining price stability. That was the thread that ran through every discussion which I had or Secretary Goldberg had. We never at any time asked for a commitment in regard to the terms, precise terms of the agreement, from either Mr. McDonald or Mr. Blough, representing the steel company, because in our opinion that would be passing over the line of propriety. But I don't think that there was any question that our great interest in attempting to secure the kind of settlement that was finally secured was to maintain price stability, which we regard as very essential at this particular time. That agreement provided the price stability up until yesterday. . . .

Q. Mr. President, on your statement on the steel industry, sir, you mentioned a number of instances which would indicate that the cost of living will go up for many people if this price increase were to remain effective. In your opinion, does that give the steelworkers the right to try to obtain some kind of a wage increase to catch up?

THE PRESIDENT: Rather interestingly, the last contract was signed on Saturday at Great Lakes so that the steel union is bound for a year, and of course, I am sure would have felt like going much further if the matters had worked out as we all hoped. But they have made their agreement and I am sure they are going to stick with it, but it does not provide for the sort of action you have mentioned.

Q. Still on steel, Senator Gore advocated today legislation to regulate steel prices somewhat in the manner that public utilities prices are regulated and his argument seemed to be that the steel industry had sacrificed some of the privileges of the free market because it wasn't really setting its prices on supply and demand, but what he called "administered prices." Your statement earlier, and your remarks since, indicate a general agreement with that kind of approach. Is that correct?

THE PRESIDENT: No, Mr. Morgan, I don't think that I have stated that. I would have to look and see what Senator Gore has suggested. I am not familiar with it. What I said was that we should examine what can be done to try to minimize the impact on the public interest of these decisions, although we had, of course, always hoped that those involved would recognize that. I would say that what must disturb Senator Gore and Congressman Celler and others, and Senator Kefauver, will be the suddenness by which every company in the last few hours, one by one as the morning went by, came in with their almost, if not identical, almost identical price increases which isn't really the way we expect the competitive private enterprise system to always work. . . .

"Police State" Methods: A Republican View

We, the members of the Joint Senate-House Republican Leadership, deplore the necessity for issuing this statement, but the issues involved are too compelling to be ignored.

Beyond the administrative operations of the Federal Government, it is a proper function of a President, in fact it is a duty, to help American private enterprise maintain a stable economy. In our free society he must usually find his way by persuasion and the prestige of his office.

Last week President Kennedy made a determination that a 3½ per cent increase [in the price of steel would] throw the American economy out of line on several fronts. In the next twenty-four hours the President directed or supported a series of Governmental actions that imperiled basic American rights, went far beyond the law, and were more characteristic of a police state than a free government.

We, the members of the Joint Senate-House Republican Leadership, believe that a fundamental issue has been raised: should a President of the United States use the enormous powers of the Federal Government to blackjack any segment of our free society into line with his personal judgment without regard to law?

SEE CUMULATIVE EFFECT

Nine actions which followed President Kennedy's press conference of Wednesday, April 11, were obviously a product of White
House direction or encouragement and must be considered for their
individual and cumulative effect. They were:

1. The Federal Trade Commission publicly suggested the possibility of collusion, announced an immediate investigation and talked
of $2,000 a day penalties.

2. The Justice Department spoke threatenly of anti-trust violations and ordered an immediate investigation.

3. Treasury Department officials indicated they were at once
reconsidering the planned increase in depreciation rates for steel.

4. The Internal Revenue Service was reported making a menac-
ing move toward U.S. Steel's incentive benefits plan for its executives.

5. The Senate Antitrust and Monopoly subcommittee began sub-
poenaing records from twelve steel companies, returnable May 14.

6. The House Antitrust subcommittee announced an immediate
investigation, with hearings opening May 2.

7. The Justice Department announced it was ordering a grand
jury investigation.

8. The Department of Defense, seemingly ignoring laws requiring
competitive bidding, publicly announced it was shifting steel purchases to companies that had not increased prices, and other Government agencies were directed to do likewise.

9. The F. B. I. began routing newspaper men out of bed at 3:00
A.M. on Thursday, April 12, in line with President Kennedy's press
conference assertion that "we are investigating" a statement attributed to a steel company official in the newspapers.

'Naked Political Power'

Taken cumulatively these nine actions amount to a display of
naked political power never seen before in this nation.

Taken singly these nine actions are punitive, heavyhanded and
frightening.

Although the President at his press conference made it clear that "price and wage decisions in this country . . . are and ought to be freely and privately made," there was nothing in the course of action which he pursued that supported this basic American doctrine.

Indeed, if big government can be used to extra-legally reverse the economic decisions of one industry in a free economy, then it can be used to reverse the decisions of any business, big or small, of labor, of farmers, in fact, of any citizen.

Most disturbing in its implications was the use of the F. B. I. Since the days of our founding fathers, this land has been the haven of millions who fled from the feared knock on the door in the night.

We condone nothing in the actions of the steel companies except their right to make an economic judgment without massive retaliation by the Federal Government.

Temporarily President Kennedy may have won a political victory, but at the cost of doing violence to the fundamental precepts of a free society.

This nation must realize that we have passed within the shadow of police state methods. We hope that we never again step into those dark regions whatever the controversy of the moment, be it economic or political.

THE PRESIDENT'S POWER IN THE
INTERNATIONAL ARENA

*President Truman's dispatch of American armed forces to Korea pro-
voked a Senate debate on the question as to whether he was em-
powered to do so in the absence of Congressional authorization. In
1951 a joint committee of the Senate's Committee on Foreign Relations and the Committee on Armed Services approved of Truman's
action in a report calling the President the "sole organ of the Nation"
in foreign affairs. The report noted that on at least 125 instances the
President "without congressional authorization, and in the absence
of a declaration of war, has ordered the Armed Forces to take action
or maintain positions abroad. . . . In sending Armed Forces to carry
out a treaty, the President does not have to have the statutory authorization of Congress." Yet the same report concluded that whatever
the respective constitutional powers of the President and Congress,
there is a great need for close collaboration: "It will be impossible
for the President to carry out for any long period of time the objectives of our foreign policy without appropriations and authorizing
legislation of various kinds from Congress." In 1957, President
Eisenhower requested and received from Congress a resolution acknowledging the independence of Middle East nations to be vital
to the national interest of the United States and authorizing him to
use armed forces at his discretion to assist any Middle East nation
against aggression from any country controlled by international communism. In 1958, the President, in consonance with this "Eisenhower doctrine," dispatched American troops to Lebanon for reasons
explained in the following message to Congress. President Kennedy's
dispatch of troops to Laos and Viet Nam in 1962 derived its authority from his power to execute SEATO treaty obligations.*

To the Congress of the United States:

*O*N JULY 14, 1958, I received an urgent request from the President of the Republic of Lebanon that some United States Forces be stationed in Lebanon. President Chamoun stated that without an immediate showing of United States support, the government of Lebanon would be unable to survive. This request by President Chamoun was made with the concurrence of all the members of the Lebanese cabinet. I have replied that we would do this and a contingent of United States Marines has now arrived in Lebanon. This initial dispatch of troops will be augmented as required. U. S. forces will be withdrawn as rapidly as circumstances permit.

Simultaneously, I requested that an urgent meeting of the United Nations Security Council be held on July 15, 1958. At that meeting, the Permanent Representative of the United States reported to the Council the action which this Government has taken. He also expressed the hope that the United Nations could soon take further effective measures to meet more fully the situation in Lebanon. We will continue to support the United Nations to this end.

United States forces are being sent to Lebanon to protect American lives and by their presence to assist the Government of Lebanon in the preservation of Lebanon's territorial integrity and independence, which have been deemed vital to United States national interests and world peace.

About two months ago a violent insurrection broke out in Lebanon, particularly along the border with Syria which, with Egypt, forms the United Arab Republic. This revolt was encouraged and strongly backed by the official Cairo, Damascus, and Soviet radios which broadcast to Lebanon in the Arabic language. The insurrection was further supported by sizeable amounts of arms, ammunition and money and by personnel infiltrated from Syria to fight against the lawful authorities. The avowed purpose of these activities was to overthrow the

Special Message to Congress on the Sending of United States Armed Forces to Lebanon, July 15, 1958, *Public Papers of the Presidents of the United States: Dwight D. Eisenhower, 1958* (Washington: G.P.O., 1959), pp. 550-552.

legally constituted government of Lebanon and to install by violence a government which would subordinate the independence of Lebanon to the policies of the United Arab Republic.

Lebanon referred this situation to the United Nations Security Council. In view of the international implications of what was occurring in Lebanon, the Security Council on June 11, 1958 decided to send observers into Lebanon for the purpose of insuring that further outside assistance to the insurrection would cease. The Secretary General of the United Nations subsequently undertook a mission to the area to reinforce the work of the observers.

It was our belief that the efforts of the Secretary General and of the United Nations observers were helpful in reducing further aid in terms of personnel and military equipment from across the frontiers of Lebanon. There was a basis for hope that the situation might be moving toward a peaceful solution, consonant with the continuing integrity of Lebanon, and that the aspect of indirect aggression from without was being brought under control.

The situation was radically changed, however, on July 14, when there was a violent outbreak in Baghdad, in nearby Iraq. Elements in Iraq strongly sympathetic to the United Arab Republic seem to have murdered or driven from office individuals comprising the lawful government of that country. We do not yet know in detail to what extent they have succeeded. We do have reliable information that important Iraqi leaders have been murdered.

We share with the Government of Lebanon the view that these events in Iraq demonstrate a ruthlessness of aggressive purpose which tiny Lebanon cannot combat without further evidence of support from other friendly nations.

After the most detailed consideration, I have concluded that, given the developments in Iraq, the measures thus far taken by the United Nations Security Council are not sufficient to preserve the independence and integrity of Lebanon. I have considered, furthermore, the question of our responsibility to protect and safeguard American citizens in Lebanon of whom there are about 2,500. Pending the taking of adequate measures by the United Nations, the United States will be acting pursuant to what the United Nations Charter recognizes is an inherent right—the right of all nations to work together and to seek help when necessary to preserve their independence. I repeat that we wish to withdraw our forces as soon as the United Nations has taken further effective steps designed to safeguard Lebanese independence.

It is clear that the events which have been occurring in Lebanon represent indirect aggression from without, and that such aggression endangers the independence and integrity of Lebanon.

It is recognized that the step now being taken may have serious consequences. I have, however, come to the considered and sober conclusion that despite the risks involved this action is required to support the principles of justice and international law upon which peace and a stable international order depend.

Our Government has acted in response to an appeal for help from a small and peaceful nation which has long had ties of closest friendship with the United States. Readiness to help a friend in need is an admirable characteristic of the American people, and I am, in this message, informing the Congress of the reasons why I believe that the United States could not in honor stand idly by in this hour of Lebanon's grave peril. As we act at the request of a friendly government to help it preserve its independence and to preserve law and order which will protect American lives, we are acting to reaffirm and strengthen principles upon which the safety and security of the United States depend.

DWIGHT D. EISENHOWER

IV. The National Legislature

THE REPUBLICAN-DIXIECRAT

COALITION

Some analysts of American politics have observed that since Franklin Roosevelt's second term, the two major parties of the United States are the Presidential Party (liberal) and the Anti-Presidential or Congressional Party (conservative). The Republican and Democratic party labels are certainly misleading except perhaps in Presidential elections. In Congress where the Democrats include Humphrey and Eastland and the Republicans Case and Goldwater, real party politics has little to do with nominal party affiliations. In the following speech by Representative Frank Thompson, Jr., of New Jersey (Democrat), the majority party in Congress is revealed as the conservative coalition between the Republicans and the Southern Democrats who tend to oppose Presidential policies particularly in domestic affairs.

MR. THOMPSON OF NEW JERSEY . . . .

*T*HE GENTLEMAN from Missouri seems to have some doubt in his mind about the existence of a coalition between Republicans and some southern Democrats here in the House. . . .

Based on last year's analysis, the average House Republican voted with the coalition 82 percent of the time on these coalition rollcall votes. Republicans and Southern Democrats hold 264 seats in the House, 45 more than a constitutional majority needed to pass or defeat any bill.

Representative Thompson (N. J.), in the *Congressional Record*, 86th Congress, 2nd session, vol. 106 (Jan. 27, 1960), pp. 1441-1442.

The operation of the coalition is a matter of record and has been most successful on legislation such as education, social welfare, public housing, immigration, taxes, labor antitrust, civil rights, public works, and resource development.

Mr. Speaker, I include at this point in the RECORD a research paper on this subject which reviews the history of the Republican-southern Democratic coalition in the House from 1937 to 1959:

The Republican-Southern Democratic coalition, or conservative coalition, as it is sometimes called, has exerted vast influence over the outcome of various types of legislation since its loose formation 22 years ago.

The 1st session of the 86th Congress saw a tightening of the coalition's voting alliance under the leadership of Minority Leader HALLECK and Judge SMITH, chairman of the House Rules Committee.

The scope and effectiveness of the coalition as described in this study is limited to legislation reaching the House floor, where its impact can be measured by analysis of rollcall votes. Of course, much of the important work of the coalition takes place in standing committees, and particularly in the House Rules Committee, where many measures are pigeonholed or watered down before a rule is granted. These aspects of coalition activity are not subject to the same type of precise analysis.

The purpose of this study is to analyze the party lineup in the 86th Congress and to briefly review the history of the Republican-Southern Democratic coalition since its beginnings in 1937 so that its operation in the present Congress may be placed in proper perspective.

The 86th Congress—Basic Arithmetic

An understanding of the role of the coalition in the 86th Congress must begin with an analysis of the real party alinement in the House. On paper it would appear that the Democratic majority in the House is the largest since New Deal days—280 Democrats, 152 Republicans. The party lineups are:

Southern Democrats................. 104
Border Democrats.................... 24
Northern and western Democrats....... 152
Republicans 152
                                    ────
Total...................... [1]432

But on the basis of three key rollcall votes in the first session on which the conservative coalition achieved its maximum strength (Thomas amendment—housing bill financing; H.R. 3—States rights issue; Landrum-Griffin substitute—labor bill), the approximate real party alinement is:

Coalition

Southern Democrats.................. 80
Border Democrats.................... 9
Northern and western Democrats........ 6
Republicans 130
                                    ────
Total........................ 225

Liberals

Southern Democrats.................. 20
Border Democrats.................... 15
Northern and western Democrats....... 143
Republicans 18
                                    ────
Total........................ 196

Absentees and vacancies, 16.

The Conservative Coalition, 1959

A Congressional Quarterly study of Republican-Southern Democrats voting alinements during the first session of the 86th Congress shows that a majority of both groups opposed a majority of northern and western Democrats on 11 of the 87 House rollcall votes. The coalition won on 10 of the 11, or 91 percent. By comparison, the coa-

[1] Excludes vacancies (Illinois, Ohio, New York, Pennsylvania).

lition won on 64 percent of the showdown votes in 1958 and 81 percent in the 1957 session.

A separate Congressional Quarterly study also reveals that southerners split with the rest of the House Democrats on 23 percent of all rollcalls during the 1959 session. They included votes on such issues as housing, civil rights, taxes, labor legislation, States rights (H.R. 3), farm price supports, surplus disposal policies, and Hawaiian statehood.

During the 1959 session, southern Democrats cast 82 percent of their votes with the Republicans and against the majority of their own party on these coalition rollcalls. The 12 southern Democratic committee chairmen cast 86.5 percent of their votes with the Republicans on these coalition rollcalls, only 10 percent with the majority of their own party.

On these same votes, 79 percent of the northern and western Democratic votes were cast with the party majority. Republicans cast 88 percent of their votes with southerners on these key rollcalls, only 9 percent with northern and western Democrats.

Coalition voting frequency would have been [even] greater if the House Rules Committee had permitted such measures as the area redevelopment bill, the civil rights bill, and Federal aid school bill to reach the House floor.

The Coalition Germinates: 1937

Beginnings of the Republican-Southern Democratic coalition in Congress can be traced back to 1937, the 1st session of the 75th Congress.

Franklin Roosevelt had just won his landslide reelection victory over Alf Landon and Democrats controlled the House by a 333 to 89 margin. Major New Deal reform measures were already on the statute books and the overwhelming Democratic victory in 1936 had provided a clear mandate for the Roosevelt administration to continue its New Deal reform and economic recovery programs.

But there were rumblings of discontent among powerful conservative forces in the Nation. The Supreme Court had already ruled several New Deal programs unconstitutional. Southerners were smarting over the repeal of the two-thirds nominating rule at the 1936 Democratic Convention, which denied them their traditional veto power over presidential choices. Resentment against the White House efforts to pack the Supreme Court began to grow in Congress.

On the national scene, organized labor was beginning to assert itself as an economic force, aided by enactment of the Wagner and Walsh-Healy Acts. Sitdown strikes became a new economic weapon in the hands of unions. Organizational strikes were being conducted in the basic industries. However, the Liberty League was strongly resisting these inroads and confidently expected the Supreme Court to rule the Wagner Act unconstitutional in a test case.

When the Court upheld the act in April 1937, it became clear to many conservatives in the industrial North and the low-wage farm areas of the South that only by forging a bipartisan conservative alliance in Congress could they hope to stem the tide of new dealism, with its growing emphasis on the needs of city dwellers, minority groups, workers, small farmers, and other underprivileged segments of the population.

This was the year that conservatives succeeded in seizing control of the House Rules Committee. They were able to change its role from that of a traffic cop in scheduling measures reported by standing committees for floor action, subject to majority leadership decisions, to that of a policy-making body—dictating to all Members which bills it deemed worthy of being considered on the House floor.

During the 1937 session, almost 10 percent of all House rollcalls showed Republicans and a majority of southern Democrats voting against a majority of Democrats from the rest of the country. Democrats divided sharply on such votes as those to authorize an investigation of sitdown strikes, on antilynching legislation, alien relief, and immigration measures. The coalition also succeeded in blocking consideration of the fair labor standards bill for the remainder of the session. However, a concerted drive by the administration resulted in passage of the bill in the second session, after it was pried out of the Rules Committee by a discharge petition.

Early Coalition Victories

During the 1st session of the 76th Congress, the coalition won two important victories—forcing an investigation of the NLRB because of alleged "prolabor" rulings and in passing the Hatch Act to prohibit political activity by Federal employees. Cleavages between northern and southern Democrats widened on such issues as housing, civil rights, labor legislation, immigration bills, relief measures, and regulation of business.

The Coalition During World War II

Although the outbreak of World War II in Europe curtailed the New Deal domestic programs, the influence of the conservative coalition continue[d] to grow. By 1941, coalition voting frequently had increased to more than 13 percent of all House rollcalls.

During the war years, the coalition succeeded in passing the Smith antistrike bill, a States rights armed services' voting bill, established the Un-American Activities Committee as a permanent House committee, and watered down the price control program and the excess profits tax measures.

By 1945, coalition voting alinements took place on 16 percent of all House rollcalls, as a combination of Rules Committee power, seniority, and attrition among northern Democrat[s] in off-year elections helped conservatives strengthen their grip on the legislative machinery of the House.

The Coalition in Postwar Years

In the immediate postwar period of the 79th Congress the coalition used its power to pass the Case strike-control bill, to exclude farm labor from NLRB jurisdiction, to turn over the U.S. Employment

Service to the States, and to take the first steps toward gutting the price control program. This latter action soon resulted in a wave of speculation, profiteering, and inflation, costing the American public billions of dollars in lost purchasing power.

After the election of the Republican 80th Congress in 1946, the coalition achieved its greatest numerical strength. It succeeded in passing the Taft-Hartley Act and in overriding President Truman's veto of the measure. It reduced coverage under the Social Security Act, overrode Truman's veto of the "rich man's" tax reduction bill, and further weakened price and rent controls.

The hand of the coalition was also seen in blocking such measures as an effective public housing program, Federal aid to education, civil rights, an increase in the minimum wage, an adequate farm program, and other legislation which President Truman proposed to the 80th Congress. His 1948 "whistle stop" campaign against the "special interests" which dominated the 80th Congress won for him his upset victory over Dewey and formed the basic planks of his Fair Deal program.

The Coalition Versus The Fair Deal

The Republican-Southern Democratic coalition in the 81st Congress was a major force in blocking enactment of important segments of the Truman legislative program and in watering down others. A majority of Republicans and southern Democrats voted together against administration proposals on about 30 percent of all substantive rollcalls in the House.

The high frequency of coalition voting is at least partially explained by the change in House rules on the opening day of the session. The House Rules Committee was stripped of its power to pigeonhole bills reported by standing committees by adoption of the 21-day rule, which permitted committee chairmen to call up bills reported by his committee, if they were not acted upon by the Rules Committee within a 21-day period. This meant that many of the controversial administration bills reached the floor for debate and vote which otherwise would have been held up in the Rules Committee.

Among the measures brought to the floor under the new 21-day rule were Hawaiian and Alaskan statehood bills, a rivers and harbors bill, the National Science Foundation bill, an antipoll tax bill, a VA hospital bill, and a joint resolution providing for U.S. participation in international organizations. In addition, the threat of using the new rule forced a reluctant Rules Committee to act on minimum wage, social security, and public housing legislation, all of which were subsequently enacted into law.

The conservative coalition did succeed in defeating an attempt to repeal the Taft-Hartley Act; in rejecting the Brannan farm plan; in permitting "local option" decontrol of rents; in defeating the National Minerals Act; in watering down the minimum wage bill; in passing the natural gas and basing point bills (both vetoed); in reducing foreign aid funds and funds for public housing; in rejecting controls over commodity speculation, and in watering-down an FEPC bill.

A coalition attempt to repeal the 21-day rule early in the 2d session of the 81st Congress failed. However, the new rule was repealed by the coalition on the opening day of the 82d Congress. Since that time, the Rules Committee has tightened its hold over the legislative machinery of the House.

The Coalition During the Eisenhower Years

During the Eisenhower administration, the coalition has continued to play a dominant role. It has won a number of important victories, including those in which it turned over offshore oil resources to a few coastal States, reduced funds for the soil conservation program, blocked liberalization of the unemployment compensation system, watered-down several public housing bills, passed the natural gas bill, defeated school construction legislation, watered-down a minimum wage bill increasing the extent of coverage, blocked an investigation of administration fiscal and monetary policies, defeated the Kennedy-

Ives labor reform bill, blocked consideration of the community facility loan program.

The coalition has also appeared on such issues as antitrust legislation, water pollution control measures, civil rights, natural resource development, public works, foreign aid, H.E.W. appropriation measures, and legislation affecting the District of Columbia.

Summary

Over the years since 1937, the Republican-Southern Democratic voting coalition has operated with varying degrees of effectiveness, being most successful on legislation dealing with education, social welfare, labor, regulation of business, public works and resource development, civil rights, immigration, taxes and other economic issues, and those where States' rights have been involved.

It is in these areas that the major differences between the Republican and Democratic parties are to be found. These are also the types of issues of such vital concern to Northern and Western Democrats in the 1960 campaign.

Scholars and political writers have attempted to explain the basis for the Republican-Southern Democratic coalition in these broad areas of legislation. Many factors have been mentioned, including the high degree of party discipline among Republicans and the correspondingly low degree of party unity, loyalty, and responsibility to the party platform among congressional Democrats from the South.

Other factors often mentioned are the procedural roadblocks in the House legislative machinery, controlled by coalition leaders; the seniority system which assures conservatives of the chairmanships of a majority of the committees and subcommittees; the one-party system in most Southern States; the lack of communication and unity of purpose among Northern and Western Democrats; the antiquated apportionment formulas in many States, which gives rural areas disproportionate representation in State legislatures and in Congress; and the basic need for a realinement of the American political party system. . . .

CONGRESSIONAL POLITICS

One of the most controversial and important bills to come before Congress in recent years is "Medicare"—medical care for the aged, financed on the insurance principle by an increase in Social Security payments. Despite the high costs of ill-health in old age, more than half of all persons over 65 who are not in institutions receive less than $1,000 annual income and have no medical insurance, while another 21% have insurance covering less than 75% of their hospital bills. The Kerr-Mills Act of 1960 created a federal grant-in-aid program for the extension or development of state medical services for the aged, but only half the states (and three account for 92% of expended funds) have adopted the program, and a "means" test excludes many of the aged from eligibility even in these. Medicare would have extended to all persons, 65 and over, in-patient hospital services and most hospital costs, nursing home services, and hospital out-patient clinic diagnostic services; the aged covered by private insurance might retain such coverage (e.g., Blue Cross) but have the bill's benefits payable by the government. Medicare was defeated in the Senate by a vote of 52-48. The majority included 17 out of 21 Southern Democrats, 4 Border Democrats, and 31 out of 36 Republicans, revealing once again the domination of the G.O.P.-Dixiecrat conservative coalition. The following selection from the Senate debate presents Senator Gale W. McGee (Dem., Wyo.) arguing in favor of the bill and Senator Gordon Allott (Rep., Col.) in opposition. The bill will undoubtedly be revived and ultimately be passed.

MR. MCGEE OF WYOMING . . . .

The proposal now before this body, to provide funds for medical care for the aged through social security, has generated one of the most active and acrimonious debates across the Nation that has occurred in many years. Unfortunately, these debates have generated considerably more heat than light. Too often we find that those entering the debate have obtained their mental exercise by jumping to conclusions. Therefore, I would like to discuss a few of the more obvious misconceptions which have obscured the real issues in the hope that we may then get to the real issue—whether or not we can devise an adequate plan to help our older citizens obtain adequate medical care.

Misconception No. 1: Most of America's 17 million seniors do not need help with their medical bills.

This is obviously a view alien to that of the majority. While it is true that much health care is provided free to those who need care for which they cannot pay, public assistance agencies, private charitable organizations, and many physicians provide free services only to the extent that they can with the limited funds available. The sad fact is that many older citizens who are sorely in need of medical care do not get it because they are too proud to ask for charity. Those who do receive paid care from public and private assistance agencies do so only after the humiliating experience of proving they are in want. And consider that people over 65 suffer twice as frequently from chronic sickness as those under 65—even excluding those who are in institutions. They spend 2½ times as many days restricted to their beds—they are forced to limit their activities due to illness six times as often. Medical costs and health needs of the aged are greater today than those of other age groups in the population, their incomes often are too low for them to purchase private health insurance. The primary social security benefit (on which most retirees must rely exclusively) averages only $73 a month. The maximum benefit for a retired couple, which only a small proportion of beneficiaries receive,

Senators McGee and Allott, in *Congressional Record*, 87th Congress, 2nd session, vol. 108 (July 9 and 13, 1962), pp. 12065-12066, 12658-12662, *passim*.

is but $180 a month. Out of these small sums must come rent, food, clothing, and other necessary expenses. There is no margin for huge medical expenses brought on by a stay in the hospital.

Opponents to this bill answer this with the suggestion that the aged should therefore look to their children or relatives for help. Families do, in fact, often provide such help. Too often, however, this burden is borne at the expense of the education and the well-being of the children and grandchildren of the elderly ill. This unfortunate fact brings a heavy cost in family harmony and in the future opportunities of the children involved; and, in many instances, the relatives themselves are totally unable to meet the heavy costs involved.

Misconception No. 2: That the Kerr-Mills bill offers adequate medical benefits.

But the Kerr-Mills law clearly spells out that each State "will furnish medical assistance to aged individuals as far as practicable under the conditions in such State." Under this law, the medical services available to eligible applicants are directly proportional to the ability of each State to purchase these services. Wealthier States like New York and Massachusetts offer more medical services than do poorer States. In no State are unlimited services available to the medically indigent aged. This bill, backed by most doctors, is proving a sad failure in most of the States that have adopted it, even in the richer and more progressive States. My home State of Wyoming, which will have an estimated aged population of 29,000 by January 1965, has not yet seen fit to adopt this law.

In short, Kerr-Mills requires a degrading poverty test; it covers only so-called charity cases; it guarantees no free choice of doctors or hospitals; its program has not been adopted by most of the States; and—most important to those of us who are economically minded—it provides a drain on the Federal Treasury with no provision to balance that drain with new revenue.

Misconception No. 3: That the social security approach to financing care for the ill and aged under the King-Anderson bill would be a step toward socialism and government control of medicine.

This is, perhaps, the most ridiculous of the arguments against medicare. Nothing could be further from the truth. The improved King-Anderson bill clearly and forcefully spells out:

"There shall be no Federal controls over or intervention in the free practice of medicine."

Socialism exists when the doctors are salaried by the Government, when the hospitals are run by the Government, and when the Government controls the personnel and facilities. The proposed program would not provide a single medical service but would only help people finance the cost of their health care—and there are even alternatives to this in the compromise bill. It would in no way control, regulate, or interfere with the practice of medicine.

The patient also is free to choose his own doctor, who in turn is free to work in the hospital of which he is a staff member. The bill further guarantees to hospitals the freedom of choice to participate in the President's proposed health care program or not.

If enacted into law, it will operate like Blue Cross with the doctors and hospitals free to disburse their services as they have done in the past. The only point of difference is the method of financing the costs of those services rendered. Instead of the individual or private insurance paying all, the social insurance trust fund will cover all or part of the allowable costs.

This health insurance is a reasonable and important part of income protection in retirement. Without such benefits the social security program cannot adequately provide basic security for the aged. This is the only way to remove the threat to the financial independence of older people posed by the high cost of illness.

Misconception No. 4: That this program would cost too much.

Under the social security insurance, under which the individual contributed during the working years when he can best afford the contributions, payments are spread out over a working lifetime and the cost to the individual is reduced to pennies a day. The program would be financed by contributions from both workers and their employers without imposing a burden on general revenues. In fact, reduction in expenditures which would otherwise be necessary by the States and Federal Government under public assistance would partially offset the cost of the new program. The cost to the Federal budget would be nil whereas under the present law the cost was $280 million in fiscal year 1961. In fiscal year 1963 it will be an estimated $412 million.

Admittedly, the social security tax will be increased by one-fourth of 1 percent and the self-employed, covered by social security, will pay an additional three-eighths of 1 percent. In dollars and cents, this one-fourth of 1 percent amounts to about $12.50 per employee per year, or $1.04 a month, or 26 cents a week—less than the price of a pack of cigarettes—and undoubtedly healthier.

Misconception No. 5: That there would be an overutilization of services.

The plan provides at least three safeguards against overutilization. First, there are the attending physicians that must certify, and at certain times recertify, that services are required for medical treatment or diagnosis.

The second safeguard is provided by the institution itself, which would review admissions, duration of stay, and services furnished.

The third safety measure is built into the program in the types of services covered and in the requirements for deductibles. Since protection is provided against the costs of outpatient diagnostic, skilled nursing home, and home health services, there will be no financial incentive to unnecessarily use higher cost services when the lower cost services will suffice. The deductibles might also tend to reduce unnecessary utilization of hospital services.

Aging is a phenomenon both personal and public, both evident and elusive. Time passes: as an experience within, as a dimension without. New forces and new problems make disturbing patterns in the latter years. The stereotypes are only too familiar: the rocking chair, the empty hands, the illnesses of age, the unwanted look, the passive posture. Are these the only meaning of being old? Too long have these misconceptions persisted. These cobwebs have ensnarled the struggling elderly, thus denying them their rightful place in the sun. Realities, if not ignored by those who do not want to admit hard truths, can bring security and peace of mind to those elderly who now face fear and deprivation as an unwelcome reward for their many years of toil.

Up to the present time, nearly all programs in behalf of the aging in the United States are the product of the welfare mood and of uncritical adoption of untested projects. The proposed administration bill for aid to the aged medically indigent is not only not welfare but has been tested through long and favorable experience. The time has come for Congress to provide the insight and the law to help both the younger and an older society to act with wisdom about age.

So far the debate on this proposal, now before us, has degenerated into a picayunish business which is smothering it under a landslide of verbiage—and at a time when it desperately needs fresh air. At present there is the very real danger that this headless chase will end in a monster bill embodying just those aspects of the problem we wish to avoid.

We must not allow this comprehensive piece of legislation to be pecked to death. Rather, we must get off our petty and sometimes partisan political stumps, and provide for the urgent need of the elderly ill by passing this constructive and essential King-Anderson medical care bill, as improved, with all deliberate speed.

MR. ALLOTT OF COLORADO. . . .

What we are offered by the Anderson-Javits amendment is this: Basically, we still have the King-Anderson bill, with a few modifications. . . . The new provisions of which much is made, and which I will discuss later, are: First, to allow the Secretary of HEW in his discretion, to designate an agent, such as Blue Cross, chosen by the provider of services, to handle the administrative details in the provider's dealings with the Government; and, second, to allow the patient or beneficiary the privilege of having the benefits to which he is entitled under the bill paid to the provider—the hospital—by his own private health insurance organization such as Blue Cross; such organization would then be reimbursed by the Government.

Also, a separate trust fund for health insurance would be established.

What Is Offered and Deficiencies

Ultimately, any appraisal of merits and demerits in such widely different approaches to Government aid as Kerr-Mills Act and the Javits-Anderson bill requires that the fundamental, philosophic differences be examined carefully. These are basically three in number. Each must be studied from the viewpoint of both the immediate effect and the long-range implications. Broadly speaking, these three fundamental differences under the Javits-Anderson bill are as follows:

First. All of the beneficiaries, whether they be under social security or not, would receive aid regardless of need.

Second. Care would be limited to (a) a specific number of days in the hospital and nursing homes; (b) physician diagnostic services provided through hospital clinic; and (c) services of the home health agencies, which must be a nonprofit corporation or a public agency.

Excluded would be (a) drugs, except those provided in one of the above-cited institutions; (b) private physician services in or out of the institution; and (c) nursing or other professional services except those provided through one of the above cited institutions.

Third. Administration of the program, for all practical purposes, would be by the Federal Government in Washington.

It is in these three areas of conflict that the fundamental issues regarding Government's role in medical care for older people are to be found.

Anderson-Javits Substitutes Government Care For Private Initiative

In direct contrast with the Kerr-Mills Act, the Anderson-Javits approach would provide limited help to everyone over 65 covered by social security, plus approximately 2,500,000 persons not covered by social security, whether such persons in either instance need or want help or not . . . . Even millionaires would be recipients of aid. The disregard of the need factor by the Anderson-Javits bill is important in its immediate effects. Most obvious is the unnecessary cost to the taxpayer providing services for those who are able and willing to accept personal responsibility for meeting their own needs. Equally important is the virtually complete destruction of a substantial portion of the voluntary health insurance effort which is rapidly responding to the needs of older people.

Immediate effects, however, are insignificant when compared with the possibilities of the future. Historically, there has been a tendency for age requirements to be lowered once a program of this type gets underway. While social security benefits are not technically a matter of legal right for those who have paid their social security taxes, they are generally so regarded by the individuals paying such taxes. It is quite reasonable to assume that this belief in their right might reinforce efforts for age requirements, eventually completely destroying the private enterprise system of medical care now enjoyed by the American people. That such a possibility is real, is underscored by the fact that many of the prime movers for King-Anderson, and now Anderson-Javits, have long advocated total, compulsory Federal health care for the whole population.

In the United States as elsewhere, Government very definitely operates on precedent. Once the precedent is established under the Anderson-Javits, or a similar bill, that medical care should be provided to individuals without regard for need, no matter how few the number or how limited the benefits, it will be a simple matter to extend such assistance to increasingly large numbers, conceivably to all of the people. The dangers of such an extension are especially real under the social security tax method of financing such assistance. Since working people will be paying the bill, it is almost inevitable that many of them will want to share in the benefits. Former Congressman Forand, author of a previously rejected bill similar to the King-Anderson bill, has said:

> If we can only break through and get our foot inside the door, then we can expand the program after that.

. . . If the dollars now provided by the social security system are replaced with medical services—because someone in Government has decided that that is what older people need—it is illogical to stop there.

Why should not the noncash principle be extended to food, clothing, shelter, and other necessities?

Some of the people advocating the social security approach would like to greatly expand public housing for older persons. In both the executive and legislative branches there is considerable discussion of what constitutes "proper housing" for older people. It implies that Government should decide what housing is needed whether it really meets the desires of older people or not.

These bureaucracy builders are strangely disinclined to provide equivalent amounts of cash which people could spend as they, themselves, choose.

Government involvement in activities which should be left to individual initiative, private enterprise, and voluntary action is dangerous to the Nation's future. For, while socialization of part of medical care has been followed by total socialized medicine, even more serious is the historical fact that socialized medicine has been but a beginning of nationalization of other fields. . . .

It is further said that being a contributory program the social security approach would place no load on the Federal budget, but that it would, in fact, help balance it.

The significant thing to keep in mind in meeting the costs of Government activities is whether such costs are to be met through taxes, inflation, or through other methods, all of which confiscate part of the individual's assets or earnings.

I suggest, Mr. President, although the employer under social security contributes an equal amount to that which the employee contributes, this comes from the net earnings of the corporation. It is a fact ordinarily overlooked that to such an extent this eliminates from the net earnings of the corporation a portion which might otherwise be shared with the employee.

The social security system and other self-financing programs such as the highway trust fund do not appear in what is usually referred to as the Federal budget, but this is purely an administrative device.

Special taxes, such as those under social security, are actually no different from other taxes; except, possibly, as to the method of levy. Expenditures under such special programs are equally no different in their effects on the economy.

Obviously, if costs are high, they not only reduce the freedom of individuals to spend their money, but also impair the ability of States and communities to gain public acceptance of taxes needed to pay for their programs.

Cost Factors And Estimates Involved In Anderson-Javits Amendment

I would like to take a moment to discuss the cost factors and estimates involved in the Anderson-Javits amendment. . . . I believe these estimates to be totally unrealistic for the following reasons: I believe the estimates are understated because: First, they understate the number of aged persons not eligible for either OASI or railroad retirement benefits; second, they understate the cost of providing health benefits to each person eligible under the provision of the amendment; third, they overstate the savings which the Government would realize under this new public assistance and veterans programs. . . . I estimate the net cost to the Federal Government for providing health benefits to the non-OASI population to be $265 million in 1964. There is a likelihood that this figure could well be in excess of one-third of a billion. . . .

Also, in view of the underestimation of the cost of the envisaged program by the Department of Health, Education, and Welfare, and consequently the underestimation of required revenue to finance the program, the conclusion is inescapable that the proposed increase in the social security tax will only be a first installment increase. More hikes must occur.

Anderson-Javits Does Not Meet Older People's Needs

The second fundamental difference the Kerr-Mills Act and the Anderson-Javits approach makes, is that the latter would provide limited services which might, or might not meet the pressing medical and financial assistance needs of the patient. . . .

Anderson-Javits Concentrates Power In Central Government

The third major difference between the present law and the Anderson-Javits approach revolves around the question of whether the administration should be by State and community, as under the Kerr-Mills Act, or by the Federal Government. Congress has long acted on the precedent of grants and aid to States as the proper governmental technique in providing services to individual citizens who need them. This principle is inherent in the present law as set forth in the Kerr-Mills Act. Adoption of Anderson-Javits would be in direct violation of this precedent with most serious implications for the Nation's whole governmental system.

Much more is at stake here than a simple matter of administrative techniques. The whole doctrine of separation of governmental powers, as worked out by the Founding Fathers and reaffirmed by succeeding generations, is at issue.

Adoption of the Anderson-Javits approach would be more than a "foot in the door" for socialized medicine; it would be a long step toward the creation of a new and all-powerful Federal bureaucracy in Washington with a corollary destruction of significant authority and responsibility by State and local government.

In the field of health, itself, the present participation by the Federal Government is limited. If the principles in the Anderson-Javits bill are accepted, they could equally apply to public health measures. If the States are deemed incompetent in provision of medical care to individuals in need, why shouldn't they be deemed incompetent to conduct administration of public health activities? The latter much more clearly affect the total population. They far more certainly cross

State lines in their several implications. Are State and local health departments to be replaced by a Federal health juggernaut?

This question is not confined solely to health or medical care. In its large implications, it must be viewed in the total context of possible changes in America's Government. There seems to be a substantial group of people who want to destroy the traditional division of powers, replacing them with centralized concentration of control far removed from the people.

The Kennedy administration has given encouragement to this point of view. Two recent examples should suffice: First, the unsuccessful recommendation that Congress surrender to the executive its control over taxes; and second, the unsuccessful effort to increase Federal involvement in local and State affairs through the proposed creation of a Department of Urban Affairs and Housing, which would have responsibility for certain types of activities in all communities of more than 2,500 population—using definition of "urban population" used by U.S. Bureau of the Census.

The differences between the Kerr-Mills law and the Anderson-Javits approach regarding further extension of Federal control are obvious. . . .

Much ado has been made over the provisions now added in the Anderson-Javits amendment, not present in the original King-Anderson bill, which would first, allow the Secretary of Health, Education, and Welfare in his discretion, to designate an agent, such as Blue Cross, chosen by the provider of services, to handle the administrative details in the provider's dealings with the Government; and second, allow the patient or beneficiary the privilege of having the benefits to which he is entitled under the bill paid to the provider— the hospital—by his own private health insurance organization such as Blue Cross; such organization would then be reimbursed by the Government.

The only result of these provisions is this: The Secretary of Health, Education, and Welfare, in the first instance, while authorized to enter into agreements with these organizations to handle certain administrative details and act as intermediaries between the providers and the Government, is under no compulsion to do so. Such a relationship, even if made, is of course under the strict guidance and control of the Secretary and the Department as it inevitably must be when solely Federal funds are being dispensed. . . .

V. The Restraints Imposed by Law

CIVIL RIGHTS

The Civil Rights Act of 1957 authorized the establishment of a bi-
partisan Commission on Civil Rights. Powerless to enforce laws or
correct any wrongs, the Commission can investigate complaints that
citizens are being deprived of their right to vote by reason of their
race, religion, or national origin; gather and study information con-
cerning denials of equal protection of the laws under the Constitution
and appraise the laws and policies of the national government re-
specting equal protection; and report its findings and recommenda-
tions to the President and Congress. In 1961 the Commission, under
the chairmanship of John A. Hannah, president of Michigan State
University, issued a monumental five-volume report that surveyed
civil rights in the fields of voting, education, employment, housing,
and justice. The following selection is from the introduction of that
report.

*I*N war and peace the American people have met challenge after
challenge with vigor and resourcefulness. Perhaps the most persistent
challenge is the one to which this Commission addresses itself in this
report—the challenge of civil rights.

The Republic began with an obvious inconsistency between its
precepts of liberty and the fact of slavery. The words of the Declaration of Independence were clear:

We hold these truths to be self-evident, that all men are created equal,
that they are endowed by their Creator with certain unalienable rights,

1961 United States Commission on Civil Rights Report (Washington: G.P.O., 1961),
vol. 1, *Voting*, pp. 1-13.

that among these are Life, Liberty, and the Pursuit of Happiness. That to secure these rights, Governments are instituted among Men, deriving their just powers from the consent of the governed.

Equally clear was the fact that Negroes were not free. The great American experiment in self-government began for white people only.

The inconsistency between the Nation's principles and its practices has diminished over the years. Constitutional amendments, court decisions, acts of Congress, Executive orders, administrative rulings, State and local legislation, the work of private agencies, efforts by Negroes and other minority groups—all these have helped remove many of the barriers to full citizenship for all.

The gains have been considerable. As the second term of this Commission draws to a close, it can report that more persons than ever before are exercising more fully their rights as citizens of the United States. The American people are increasingly aware that professions of belief in the dignity of man have meaning only if they are realized by all people in all aspects of life. The gap between the promise of liberty and its fulfillment is narrower today that it has ever been.

Yet a gap remains. In the changing world of 1961 it seems wide and deep, and the demand to close it is more urgent than ever. Perhaps this is because the closer we come to the achievement of our ideals, the more obvious and galling is the remaining disparity. Partly, too, events in a rapidly changing world have put a new focus on the way in which the United States puts its principles into practice. The emergence of new nonwhite nations in Africa and Asia does not make an inequity any more unjust. It may, however, make remedial action more urgent.

The report that follows attempts to measure the remaining gap between the American promise and its fulfillment; to tell of progress that has been made, and to suggest approaches for what remains to be done.

This report principally concerns the civil rights problems of Negroes. Mexican-Americans, Puerto Ricans, Indians, and other minorities to some extent still suffer inequalities and deprivation.

But Negroes are our largest minority group, and their rights are denied more often in more respects and in more places than are those of any other group. Of all minorities, Negroes seem most closely bound to the history and conscience of America. Their struggle has become symbolic. By measuring the extent to which they enjoy civil rights, we may measure our respect for freedom. To the extent that this Nation can successfully resolve its racial problems, it lends hope to afflicted minorities and troubled majorities everywhere. For this Nation is concerned not just with the civil rights of a particular minority. It is concerned with human rights for all men everywhere.

Progress During the Last Two Years

The 2 years since the Commission submitted its first report have brought dynamic changes in civil rights at all levels of government. These are some of the milestones of progress on the national level:
• In 1960 Congress passed the second Civil Rights Act since 1875, strengthening the measures available to the Federal Government for dealing with such matters as discriminatory denials of the right to vote, obstruction of Federal court orders, and bombing or other desecration of schools and churches.
• Through the courts the Federal Government acted energetically to secure the constitutional rights of its citizens against invasion by the States: it brought suits to protect the right of Negroes to vote without discrimination or coercion on account of race in 15 counties in Alabama, Louisiana, Georgia, Mississippi, and Tennessee; in New Orleans it intervened in a school desegregation suit to protect its courts and its citizens against State defiance of the law of the land; in Montgomery, Ala., it sued to protect the right of Americans to travel freely among the States, without distinction or obstruction because of their race; again in New Orleans, and in Montgomery, it sued to end segregation in airport facilities built in part with Federal funds; in Jackson, Miss., it intervened in a suit to restrain arrests of persons seeking unsegregated service in bus terminals; in Biloxi, Miss., it brought suit to assure that a public beach constructed with funds from

the National Government would be available to all the public without racial discrimination.

• With the creation of the President's Committee on Equal Employment Opportunity in 1961, the executive branch of the Federal Government took a major step to achieve the national policy that there shall be no discrimination on grounds of race, color, creed, or national origin, either in employment by the Government itself, or in employment created by funds dispensed from the National Treasury.

• The President of the United States publicly affirmed his support of the Supreme Court's decision that segregated public schools were forbidden by the Constitution.

• The Supreme Court, followed by the lower Federal courts, has firmly upheld constitutional and statutory commands against discrimination in this period:

It held in 1961 that a State could not redraw municipal boundary lines on racial grounds.

In 1961 it held that the operation of a private restaurant in space leased from a public agency was State action within the meaning of the 14th amendment; and that the facility, therefore, could not be operated on a discriminatory basis.

In 1960 it held that Congress had forbidden racial segregation in services provided for interstate travelers even if the services are not provided directly by an interstate carrier itself.

Also in 1960 it upheld the 1957 Civil Rights Act against constitutional attack.

• State and local governments also took important steps:

Twenty-three State laws aimed at preventing racial or religious discrimination in such areas as housing, employment, and public accommodations were enacted or strengthened—not only in Northern and Western States but in border States such as Kentucky, West Virginia, Delaware, Missouri, and Kansas.

In the deeper South, Georgia followed the example of Virginia in abandoning massive resistance to the requirements of the Constitution regarding public education. The first public educational institution in Georgia—the University of Georgia—was successfully desegregated with only temporary difficulty, and preparations were made for the orderly advent of desegregation in the Atlanta public schools. Thus, all but three States (Alabama, Mississippi, and South Carolina) had made at least some progress toward the constitutional operation of public schools and colleges. A handful of school districts in the South passed quietly and without difficulty from segregation into a program of compliance with the Constitution.

With or without lawsuits, public libraries, parks, and recreation facilities were successfully desegregated in a number of southern cities.

• Perhaps the most important events of the period, however, were brought about by private citizens:

On February 1, 1960, four freshmen students from the North Carolina Agricultural & Technical College entered a variety store in Greensboro, made several purchases, then sat down at the lunch counter and ordered coffee. They were refused service because they were Negroes, but they remained in their seats until the store closed. Thus began the sit-in movement, a movement of protest mainly by Negro youth. It spread rapidly through the South and even to some places in the North, manifesting itself as well in other forms of peaceful protest—kneel-ins, stand-ins, wade-ins, and more recently and spectacularly in the "Freedom Rides." This protest movement has aroused widespread interest and strong feelings. Although doubts of its wisdom and concern as to its methods are genuinely felt by many, there can be no question that its moral impetus is strong, that it expresses a profound and widespread demand for faster realization of equal opportunity for Negroes, or that it will continue until the issues raised by its demands have been resolved.

Partly as a result of the sit-ins, there has been a marked change, for the most part unpublicized and without drama, in many southern cities. Racial barriers have been removed not only in areas where the law of the land supported the claim for equal treatment—as in publicly operated facilities and interstate transportation terminals—but also in many areas of private concern where no legal compulsion has been held to exist. By the close of 1960, for instance, variety store chains had opened lunch counters in 112 southern and border cities to Negro patrons.

Equally important has been the growing awareness among thoughtful southern white leaders of the dimensions of civil rights problems. James J. Kilpatrick, a Virginian, editor of the Richmond News-Leader, and one of the earliest proponents of massive resistance to school desegregation, spoke for many when he said:

> What I am groping to say is that many a southerner is seeing now, and hearing now. Aspects of segregation that once were his nonconcern now trouble his spirit uncomfortably: Sit-ins. Segregated libraries. Certain job discrimination. Genuinely unequal schools in some areas. The Negro as citizen, as a political being possessed of equal rights, never had existed in the white southerner's past as he begins to exist now. The familiar black faces, seen through new glasses, are startlingly unfamiliar. A sense of the Negro point of view, totally unrecognized before, stirs uneasily in the conscious mind. . . .

That Mr. Kilpatrick spoke for many responsible white southerners is confirmed by their effective efforts in such vital spots as Little Rock, Atlanta, and New Orleans to keep public schools open, even if it meant desegregation. A number of church and other organizations throughout the South have decried the immorality of all forms of racial discrimination.

In the North and West as well, private groups have become increasingly active in expressing by action as well as words a belief in equal treatment regardless of race, creed, or ancestry.

Problems Still Unsolved

Despite this progress, however, the Nation still faces substantial and urgent problems in civil rights. It is with these that the Commission, by virtue of its statutory directive, has been principally concerned. Among the major civil rights problems discussed in the report that follows are these:

In some 100 counties in eight Southern States there is reason to believe that Negro citizens are prevented—by outright discrimination or by fear of physical violence or economic reprisal—from exercising the right to vote.

There are many places throughout the country where, though citizens may vote freely, their votes are seriously diluted by unequal electoral districting, or malapportionment.

There are many counties in the South where a substantial Negro population not only has no voice in government, but suffers extensive deprivation—legal, economic, educational, and social.

There are still some places in the Nation where the fear of racial violence clouds the atmosphere. There is reason to hope that the worst form of such violence—lynching—has disappeared; no incidents have occurred during the last 2 years. Still, mob violence has erupted several times in response to the campaign for recognition of Negro rights—in Jacksonville, Fla., and New Orleans, La.; in Anniston, Montgomery, and Birmingham, Ala.; in Chicago, Ill.

Unlawful violence by the police remains in 1961 not a regional but a national shame.

In public education there still are three States—Alabama, Mississippi, and South Carolina—where not one public school or college conforms with the constitutional requirements enumerated by the Supreme Court 7 years ago. In May 1961, 2,062 of the 2,837 biracial school districts in the 17 Southern and border States remained totally segregated.

Perhaps even more serious is the threat posed by a new southern strategy of avoiding the full impact of constitutional commands by withdrawing the State from public education.

One Southern State, Louisiana, not only set itself in defiance of constitutional requirements in public education, but attempted to "interpose" its authority against the Federal Constitution, and obstruct the processes of the National Government. Its legislature passed no fewer than 56 laws for these purposes—25 of which were struck down quickly by the Federal courts. Other Louisiana laws, all part of a "segregation package," were intended to diminish Negro voting; to inhibit protest demonstrations; to deprive thousands of children, mainly Negro, of welfare assistance.

A Federal court decision in 1961 brought to the Nation's attention the fact that unconstitutional inequality in public education is not confined to Southern States. Such inequalities in public educational systems seem to exist in many cities throughout the Nation.

Unemployment in the recent recession, hitting Negroes more than twice as hard as others, underlined the fact that they are by and large confined to the least skilled, worst paid, most insecure occupations; that they are most vulnerable to cyclical and structural unemployment and least prepared to share in, or contribute to, the economic progress of the Nation.

Although racial segregation in the Armed Forces of the United States officially ended 6 years ago, it continues in some parts of the Reserves and the National Guard.

Much of the housing market remains closed in 1961 to millions of Americans because of their race, their religion, or their ancestry; and partly in consequence millions are confined to substandard housing in slums.

In spite of repeated commitments to the principle that benefits created by the funds of all the people shall be available to all without regard to race, religion, or national ancestry, the Federal Government continues in some programs to give indirect support to discriminatory practices in higher education, in training programs, in employment agencies and opportunities, in public facilities such as libraries, and in housing.

Nature of the Problems

These are the principal civil rights problems the Commission has found in the areas it has undertaken to study—voting, education, employment, housing, and administration of justice. In dealing with these subjects, however, the Commission has attempted to define and measure civil rights deprivations, and to put them in proper context.

First of all there are the commands of the Nation's Constitution, based on principles which go to the roots of a free society. Even where the writ of the Constitution itself does not run, goals and policies of equal opportunity have often been set by the people through their National Government. While the principle behind the constitutional, statutory, and executive directives is clear—recognition of the worth of every human being—their application is sometimes difficult; for civil rights issues are often closely related to other serious national problems. One of these is the problem of bringing into the mainstream of American life large groups of people suffering from serious deprivations. Also contributing to the complexity of civil rights problems is the fact that while they occur throughout the Nation, and not in any one region alone, they take somewhat different forms in the South and the North, and in rural and urban areas. Finally, civil rights difficulties are complicated by the division of private and governmental responsibilities within our Federal system. Preliminary discussion of these complex interrelated issues may provide perspective for the report that follows.

THE COMMAND OF NONDISCRIMINATION

The 15th amendment to the Constitution commands that neither the Federal Government nor the States may deny or abridge the right to vote on account of race or color. More broadly, the 14th amendment forbids any State or its agents to "deny to any person the equal protection of the laws." This principle, applicable also to the Federal Government, forbids discrimination against any person on grounds of race, color, religion, or national origin. It does not reach the conduct of persons acting in a purely private capacity. Still, a State may not enforce private agreements to discriminate; and in some circumstances private persons may act under the authority of the State and bring themselves within the constitutional prohibition. How much aid, direction, or control by a State is required to invoke the constitutional ban against discrimination is still largely undefined.

It is now clear that the discrimination forbidden by the Constitution includes not only tangibly unequal treatment but, in many if not all fields, the intangible inequality of enforced segregation. The doctrine of "separate but equal" has been struck down not only in public education but in public transportation, and public recreational facilities such as parks, golf courses, and swimming pools.

Although the Constitution forbids Government to discriminate, or to enforce private discrimination, it has not authoritatively been held to forbid either Federal or State Government indirectly to *assist* others in discriminating. In fact the Federal Government gives many kinds of financial or other assistance to private persons and groups, and even State agencies, which discriminate on racial, religious, or ethnic grounds. If this does not necessarily raise constitutional problems, it raises serious questions of national policy.

While the Commission has not systematically studied all Federal programs in which these questions arise, several of the studies reported below do pose the problem: Should the Federal Government allow its funds and benefits to be used in such a way that some people are denied enjoyment thereof solely on grounds of race or creed? In several cases the answer has already been given in declarations either by Congress or by the President that the policy of the Nation is one of equality of opportunity for all. One of the Commission's major concerns has been to measure the consistency and effectiveness of such laws and policies of the Federal Government.

PROBLEMS OF CUMULATIVE DEPRIVATION

Civil rights problems do not arise in the abstract. The Commission is aware that those who are denied their constitutional rights are usually also the victims of poverty and inadequate formal education. Particularly since World War I the underprivileged have been moving into our great urban centers—in search of opportunity. The problems that they meet there are not entirely new. The history of the United States after all provides a magnificent record of absorption of vast migrations of oppressed people; the Nation has given richly to them and been richly rewarded. Today's minorities—the Negro moving from sharecropping to the city, the Puerto Rican, the Mexican-American, and the American Indian leaving the reservation—are in a sense modern immigrants seeking their places in the mainstream of American life.

Like earlier immigrants from overseas, many of today's largely native-born minorities have been forced into urban slums, restricted to the poorest schools, and employed in the lowest paid occupations. Inevitably in their adjustment to city life under such handicaps, they have required a disproportionate share of health, welfare, police, and other services, and have been more vulnerable to personal and social maladjustment. As with earlier groups, these deprivations have led to discrimination, which in turn reinforces the deprivations.

While many of these problems are similar to those of other minorities, there are important differences. The Negro is no stranger to this country: he is an American by birth and by long ancestry. But he is set apart by the color of his skin. Moreover, many of his hardships are the bitter fruit of past denials of civil rights in this country. And the cumulative effect of these denials has produced a new deprivation —debilitation of hope and ambition—so that even opportunities that are available sometimes go unused. In contrast to the conviction of earlier immigrants that they—or their children—could work their way up from poverty and slums, "the outstanding characteristics of youth in the Negro slum is an almost complete lack of conviction that life can be better." Similarly, an educator described the hopelessness that breeds in the Los Angeles Mexican-American ghetto: "Joe is going to pick fruit anyway; why should he go to high school?"

Frustration of ambition and lack of hope tend to erupt in delinquency and crime. They also threaten continued mounting costs in public services for an increasing minority that is not permitted to move upward into self-sufficiency. These are essentially "social" problems, yet they are closely, and often inextricably, linked with civil rights. They present serious obstacles to the solution of civil rights issues.

There is no precise way to measure the extent of the deprivations suffered by minority groups. Census data, however, are indicative:

Education: In 1959, 23.5 percent of nonwhites 25 years of age or over were deemed functionally illiterate (completed less than 5 years of school), compared to 6.4 percent of whites. The median number of school years completed by nonwhites 25 years old and over was 8.1, compared to 11.4 for whites. Only 20 percent of nonwhites compared to 45.3 percent of whites had high school or better education; 49.5 percent of nonwhites compared to 80.8 percent of whites had elementary school or better education.

Incomes: In 1959 the median income for male nonwhite workers was $2,844, compared to $4,902 for white male workers. Median family income was $5,643 for whites, and $2,917 for nonwhites. The median income of families in relation to the formal education of the head of the family in 1958 is shown below:

	Elementary school graduates	High school graduates	College[1]
White	$4,487	$5,742	$7,373
Nonwhite	3,316	3,929	5,654

Occupations: In 1960, 55 percent of nonwhites worked in service and laboring occupations, compared to 18 percent of whites; less than 7 percent of nonwhite males were in professional and managerial jobs, compared to almost 26 percent of whites. The 1950 census (later figures are not yet available) showed that 22.3 percent of nonwhite *college graduates* were working in laboring or service jobs, compared to 1.4 percent of whites.

Unemployment: Nonwhites have consistently experienced unemployment rates at least double those of whites:

Percent of male labor force unemployed

Year	Nonwhite	White
1957	8.4	3.7
1958	13.7	6.1
1959	11.5	4.6
1960	10.7	4.8

[1] College figures include graduates and those attending for 1-3 years; no separate figures are available for nonwhite graduates.

Housing: In 1937 President Roosevelt decried the fact that "one-third of the nation is . . . ill-housed." By 1960, housing conditions had improved considerably, but not equally for all. Fifty-seven percent of all nonwhite-occupied dwelling units were classified by the 1960 census as "dilapidated," "deteriorating," or "lacking some or all plumbing facilities"—and hence substandard—compared to 24 percent of white-occupied units in this condition.

These bleak statistics give some quantitative measure of deprivation. They do, however, suggest that denial of equal opportunity is at least partly responsible for such manifestly unequal conditions, and that these conditions necessarily raise serious obstacles to the achievement of equal opportunity.

ACHIEVING NATIONAL GOALS

Mass denials of civil rights are more than a distressing problem for the affected group—they can be obstacles to the progress of the entire Nation. The goal of equal opportunity is intertwined with national goals in such areas as education, economic development, housing, and the health of our cities.

Education and a skilled populace: Democracy depends on an educated populace. It demands that every individual have the opportunity to realize his full potential through education. President Kennedy put it briefly, "Our progress as a nation can be no swifter than our progress in education." Yet there are citizens of the Nation who suffer inferior schooling for no reason apart from race.

Related to the goal of an educated citizenry is the need for a highly trained work force with the technical skills required by a rapidly changing economy. Yet manpower specialists, studying ways to utilize American resources more effectively for vital economic and defense needs, have stated that "the single most underdeveloped human resource in the country is the Negro." The causes are manifold—discrimination, early school dropouts because of financial need or lack of motivation, inferior educational facilities—but they are all in one way or another related to unequal opportunity.

Housing and the revitalization of our cities: In 1949 Congress recognized the achievement of "a decent home and a suitable living environment for every American family" as a major national goal. In 1961 President Kennedy told Congress that "we must still redeem this pledge." But the objective cannot be realized while racial barriers keep some from obtaining decent housing.

Achievement of the national housing goal is now part of a much greater problem in which civil rights is also involved—the future of our cities. A tremendous shift in population has brought increasing numbers of people to live in the cities and their burgeoning suburbs. Whereas less than a third of the U.S. population lived in "urban" areas in 1900, almost 70 percent lived in such areas in 1960, and experts forecast the figure will reach 80 to 85 percent within the next 15 years.

Most of the Nation's great cities are suffering serious common problems of decay, slum growth, loss of middle and higher income residents to the suburbs, loss of industry and retail business, insufficient low-cost housing, inadequate educational and other services, jammed transportation systems, and declining tax revenue. At the same time the rapid increase of population in the urban areas surrounding these cities puts added pressure on their facilities without contributing much to their budgets.

Meanwhile, many cities have also experienced an explosive increase in their minority populations. While 73 percent of the Nation's Negroes lived in rural areas in 1910, more than 73 percent were urban dwellers in 1960. In the North more than 90 percent were in urban centers. The proportion of Negroes in the population of Chicago, Cleveland, New York, and Philadelphia more than doubled between 1940 and 1960; in Cleveland, Detroit, and Los Angeles it tripled; in San Francisco, it increased more than twelvefold. There is every indication that the minority proportion of most cities' population will continue to increase because of further migration, the relatively higher birth rate among nonwhites, and a continued exodus of whites to the suburbs. If present trends continue, even those cities which now have small Negro populations will have a sizable proportion within 10 or 20 years.

To a considerable degree, restrictions of opportunity for these minorities concentrating in the Nation's cities have further intensified fundamental urban problems. Denials of equal opportunity in housing, and to a lesser degree in education and employment, have accelerated the growth of new slums, retarded clearance of old ones, and endangered the success of programs for urban renewal—while requiring costly additional services and providing inadequate tax revenue to pay for them.

DIFFERING CONTEXTS

The civil rights problems involved in the growing urbanization of America are not always comparable to those found in rural areas. Restrictions on the right to vote, for instance, appear almost exclusively in the rural South. Restrictions in employment, education, housing, and administration of justice, on the other hand, occur in rural and urban settings throughout the country—though they often reveal different characteristics in the different areas.

The differing nature of civil rights problems in North and South must also be recognized. In the South race restrictions have been strongly supported by law, tradition, and popular attitudes. In the North, where Negroes until recently have been a small proportion of the total population, restrictions are not the result of law, official policy, or acknowledged tradition—indeed many cities and States have laws prohibiting discrimination. Yet discrimination persists.

The vast migration of Negroes from rural to urban areas largely has been also a migration from South to North. Today, almost half of the Nation's Negroes live outside the 11 States of the Confederacy; 50 years ago more than 80 percent lived in these 11 States. In 1960 a Northern State—New York—for the first time had a larger Negro population than any Southern State, and five northern cities had larger Negro populations than any southern city.

The rural to urban, and South to North movements suggest that the major new frontier for civil rights today is in the cities and their surrounding metropolitan areas, particularly in the urban areas of the North.

THE FEDERAL PROBLEM

One final consideration affecting action to assure equal protection of the laws is the allocation of responsibility between private and governmental action, and between levels of Government within our Federal system. Essentially, the enjoyment of equal rights and the provision of equal treatment involve individuals. If each citizen of our democracy has opportunity for "life, liberty, and the pursuit of happiness" and acknowledges no less for all others, democracy will thrive. Safeguarding these principles is the responsibility of each of us. Yet, "to secure these rights, governments were instituted among men," and today, the ability to live, eat, work, go to school, and enjoy the benefits of freedom is protected and regulated by a network of local, State, and Federal laws.

Most measures affecting the citizen in his daily life originate in the town, city, county, or State. But the Constitution clearly imposes Federal responsibility to equal protection of the law. Moreover, the Federal Government is extensively and intimately involved in the fields of education, employment, housing, and urban affairs; and the laws and policies applicable to its programs in these fields necessarily affect equality of opportunity.

This Commission is convinced that the major effort to assure civil rights must be made by private individuals and groups, and by local and State government; but the Federal Government has a heavy obligation as well. The Commission, moreover, is under specific obligation to study Federal laws and policies, and to report its findings and recommendations to the President and Congress. In this report, therefore, it has focused chiefly on the Federal responsibility for assuring equal protection of the laws.

A Challenge to Americans

The inequities discussed in this report should not be taken as an indictment but as a challenge. This Nation has always responded to any threat to our freedom from abroad, yet for more than a century we have been divided over issues of racial equality and freedom of opportunity at home. The time has now come to answer the challenge within—the denial of civil rights to Americans by other Americans.

JIM CROW AND THE CONSTITUTION

The following opinion of the Supreme Court, implementing its historic decision of 1954 (Brown v. Board of Education), was delivered unanimously at an extraordinary session of the Court amidst tension and threats; Little Rock was still the focus of world attention. Chief Justice Warren recites the essential facts leading up to the case excepting only the eleventh hour defiance and interposition of the state government. As the case was being argued before the Court, the legislature, called into special session by Governor Faubus, enacted sixteen new segregation measures intended to nullify the expected decision. On the day of the decision, September 12, 1958, Faubus closed the public schools to avert the prospect of a second year of token desegregation—eight Negro students, protected by the United States Army, had attended one formerly all-white high school the year before—and sought to lease school properties to private corporations for continued operation on a segregated basis. The lower federal courts, in compliance with the decision of the Supreme Court, responded with extraordinary injunctions against the Governor and other high state officials. In 1959 the public schools reopened on a desegregated basis. In 1962 there were seventy-seven colored children attending formerly all-white junior and senior high schools; sixty-six others who had applied were found unqualified. Elementary schools are yet to be desegregated, but no further litigation is pending and all is quiet in Little Rock. Elsewhere the progress of desegregation in the border states has been substantial, but in the deep South only token desegregation in the cities and none whatever in the public schools of Alabama, Mississippi, or South Carolina has taken place.

Although there has been more deliberation than speed, violence is at low ebb, opposition is legalistic, and the death rattle of Jim Crow draws nearer.

Cooper *v.* Aaron

Opinion of the Court by Chief Justice Warren

$\mathcal{A}$ s this case reaches us it raises questions of the highest importance to the maintenance of our federal system of government. It necessarily involves a claim by the Governor and Legislature of a State that there is no duty on state officials to obey federal court orders resting on this Court's considered interpretation of the United States Constitution. Specifically it involves actions by the Governor and Legislature of Arkansas upon the premise that they are not bound by our holding in *Brown* v. *Board of Education,* 347 US 483. . . . That holding was that the Fourteenth Amendment forbids States to use their governmental powers to bar children on racial grounds from attending schools where there is state participation through any arrangement, management, funds or property. We are urged to uphold a suspension of the Little Rock School Board's plan to do away with segregated public schools in Little Rock until state laws and efforts to upset and nullify our holding in *Brown* v. *Board of Education* have been further challenged and tested in the courts. We reject these contentions.

The case was argued before us on September 11, 1958. On the following day we unanimously affirmed the judgment of the Court of Appeals for the Eighth Circuit, . . . which had reversed a judgment of the District Court for the Eastern District of Arkansas. The District Court had granted the application of the petitioners, the Little Rock School Board and School Superintendent, to suspend for two and one-half years the operation of the School Board's court-approved de-

Cooper *v.* Aaron, 358 U. S. 1 (1958).

segregation program. In order that the School Board might know, without doubt, its duty in this regard before the opening of school, which had been set for the following Monday, September 15, 1958, we immediately issued the judgment, reserving the expression of our supporting views to a later date. This opinion of all of the members of the Court embodies those views.

The following are the facts and circumstances so far as necessary to show how the legal questions are presented.

On May 17, 1954, this Court decided that enforced racial segregation in the public schools of a state is a denial of the equal protection of the laws enjoined by the Fourteenth Amendment. *Brown* v. *Board of Education.* . . . The Court postponed, pending further argument, formulation of a decree to effectuate this decision. That decree was rendered May 31, 1955. *Brown* v. *Board of Education,* 349 US 294. . . . In the formulation of that decree the Court recognized that good faith compliance with the principles declared in *Brown* might in some situations "call for elimination of a variety of obstacles in making the transition to school systems operated in accordance with the constitutional principles set forth in our May 17, 1954, decision." The Court went on to state:

Courts of equity may properly take into account the public interest in the elimination of such obstacles in a systematic and effective manner. But it should go without saying that the vitality of these constitutional principles cannot be allowed to yield simply because of disagreement with them.

While giving weight to these public and private considerations, the courts will require that the defendants make a prompt and reasonable start toward full compliance with our May 17, 1954, ruling. Once such a start has been made, the courts may find that additional time is necessary to carry out the ruling in an effective manner. The burden rests upon the defendants to establish that such time is necessary in the public interest and is consistent with good faith compliance at the earliest practicable date. To that end, the courts may consider problems related to administration, arising from the physical condition of the school plant, the school transportation system, personnel, revision of school districts and attendance areas into compact units to achieve a system of determining admission to the public schools on a nonracial basis, and revision of local laws and regulations which may be necessary in solving the foregoing problems.

Under such circumstances, the District Courts were directed to require "a prompt and reasonable start toward full compliance," and to take such action as was necessary to bring about the end of racial segregation in the public schools "with all deliberate speed." *Ibid.* Of course, in many locations, obedience to the duty of desegregation would require the immediate general admission of Negro children, otherwise qualified as students for their appropriate classes, at particular schools. On the other hand, a District Court, after analysis of the relevant factors (which, of course, excludes hostility to racial desegregation), might conclude that justification existed for not requiring the present nonsegregated admission of all qualified Negro children. In such circumstances, however, the Court should scrutinize the program of the school authorities to make sure that they had developed arrangements pointed toward the earliest practicable completion of desegregation, and had taken appropriate steps to put their program into effective operation. It was made plain that delay in any guise in order to deny the constitutional rights of Negro children could not be countenanced, and that only a prompt start, diligently and earnestly pursued, to eliminate racial segregation from the public schools could constitute good faith compliance. State authorities were thus duty bound to devote every effort toward initiating desegregation and bringing about the elimination of racial discrimination in the public school system.

On May 20, 1954, three days after the first *Brown* opinion, the Little Rock District School Board adopted, and on May 23, 1954, made public, a statement of policy entitled "Supreme Court Decision —Segregation in Public Schools." In this statement the Board recognized that

It is our responsibility to comply with Federal Constitutional requirements and we intend to do so when the Supreme Court of the United States outlines the method to be followed.

Thereafter the Board undertook studies of the administrative problems confronting the transition to a desegregated public school system at Little Rock. It instructed the Superintendent of Schools to prepare a plan for desegregation, and approved such a plan on May 24, 1955, seven days before the second *Brown* opinion. The plan provided for desegregation at the senior high school level (grades 10 through 12) as the first stage. Desegregation at the junior high and elementary levels was to follow. It was contemplated that desegregation at the high school level would commence in the fall of 1957, and the expectation was that complete desegregation of the school system would be accomplished by 1963. Following the adoption of this plan, the Superintendent of Schools discussed it with a large number of citizen groups in the city. As a result of these discussions, the Board reached the conclusion that "a large majority of the residents" of Little Rock were of "the belief . . . that the Plan, although objectionable in principle," from the point of view of those supporting segregated schools, "was still the best for the interests of all pupils in the District."

Upon challenge by a group of Negro plaintiffs desiring more rapid completion of the desegregation process, the District Court upheld the School Board's plan. . . . The Court of Appeals affirmed. . . . Review of that judgment was not sought here.

While the School Board was thus going forward with its preparation for desegregating the Little Rock school system, other state authorities, in contrast, were actively pursuing a program designed to perpetuate in Arkansas the system of racial segregation which this Court had held violated the Fourteenth Amendment. First came, in November 1956, an amendment to the State Constitution flatly commanding the Arkansas General Assembly to oppose "in every Constitutional manner the Un-Constitutional desegregation decisions of May 17, 1954 and May 31, 1955 of the United States Supreme Court," Ark. Const. Amend. 44, and, through the initiative, a pupil assignment law. . . . Pursuant to the constitutional command, a law relieving school children from compulsory attendance at racially mixed schools . . . and a law establishing a State Sovereignty Commission . . . were enacted by the General Assembly in February 1957.

The School Board and the Superintendent of Schools nevertheless continued with preparations to carry out the first stage of the desegregation program. Nine Negro children were scheduled for admission in September 1957 to Central High School, which has more than two thousand students. Various administrative measures, designed to assure the smooth transition of this first stage of desegregation, were undertaken.

On September 2, 1957, the day before these Negro students were to enter Central High, the school authorities were met with drastic opposing action on the part of the Governor of Arkansas who dispatched units of the Arkansas National Guard to the Central High School grounds, and placed the school "off limits" to colored students. As found by the District Court in subsequent proceedings, the Governor's action had not been requested by the school authorities, and was entirely unheralded. The findings were these:

Up to this time [September 2], no crowds had gathered about Central High School and no acts of violence or threats of violence in connection with the carrying out of the plan had occurred. Nevertheless, out of an abundance of caution, the school authorities had frequently conferred with the Mayor and Chief of Police of Little Rock about taking appropriate steps by the Little Rock police to prevent any possible disturbances or acts of violence in connection with the attendance of the 9 colored students at Central High School. The Mayor considered that the Little Rock police force could adequately cope with any incidents which might arise at the opening of school. The Mayor, the Chief of Police, and the school authorities made no request to the Governor or any representative of his for State assistance in maintaining peace and order at Central High School. Neither the Governor nor any other official of the State government consulted with the Little Rock authorities about whether the Little Rock police were prepared to cope with any incidents which might arise at the school, about any need for State assistance in maintaining peace and order, or about stationing the Arkansas National Guard at Central High School. *Aaron* v. *Cooper*, 156 F. Supp. 220, 225.

The Board's petition for postponement in this proceeding states: "The effect of that action [of the Governor] was to harden the core of opposition to the Plan and cause many persons who theretofore had reluctantly accepted the Plan to believe that there was some power in the State of Arkansas which, when exerted, could nullify the Federal law and permit disobedience of the decree of this [District] Court, and from that date hostility to the Plan was increased and criticism of the officials of the [School] District has become more bitter and unrestrained." The Governor's action caused the School Board to request the Negro students on September 2 not to attend the high school "until the legal dilemma was solved." The next day, September 3, 1957, the Board petitioned the District Court for instructions, and the court, after a hearing, found that the Board's request of the Negro students to stay away from the high school had been made because of the stationing of the military guards by the state authorities. The court determined that this was not a reason for departing from the approved plan, and ordered the School Board and Superintendent to proceed with it.

On the morning of the next day, September 4, 1957, the Negro children attempted to enter the high school but, as the District Court later found, units of the Arkansas National Guard "acting pursuant to the Governor's order, stood shoulder to shoulder at the school grounds and thereby forcibly prevented the 9 Negro students . . . from entering," as they continued to do every school day during the following three weeks. . . .

That same day, September 4, 1957, the United States Attorney for the Eastern District of Arkansas was requested by the District Court to begin an immediate investigation in order to fix responsibility for the interference with the orderly implementation of the District Court's direction to carry out the desegregation program. Three days later, September 7, the District Court denied a petition of the School Board and the Superintendent of Schools for an order temporarily suspending continuance of the program.

Upon completion of the United States Attorney's investigation, he and the Attorney General of the United States, at the District Court's request, entered the proceedings and filed a petition on behalf of the United States, as *amicus curiae*, to enjoin the Governor of Arkansas and officers of the Arkansas National Guard from further attempts to prevent obedience to the court's order. After hearings on the petition, the District Court found that the School Board's plan had been obstructed by the Governor through the use of National Guard troops, and granted a preliminary injunction on September 20, 1957, enjoining the Governor and the officers of the Guard from preventing the attendance of Negro children at Central High School, and from otherwise obstructing or interfering with the orders of the court in connection with the plan. . . . The National Guard was then withdrawn from the school.

The next school day was Monday, September 23, 1957. The Negro children entered the high school that morning under the protection of the Little Rock Police Department and members of the Arkansas State Police. But the officers caused the children to be removed from the school during the morning because they had difficulty controlling a large and demonstrating crowd which had gathered at the high school. . . . On September 25, however, the President of the United States dispatched federal troops to Central High School and admission of the Negro students to the school was thereby effected. Regular army troops continued at the high school until November 27, 1957. They were then replaced by federalized National Guardsmen who remained throughout the balance of the school year. Eight of the Negro students remained in attendance at the school throughout the school year.

We come now to the aspect of the proceedings presently before us. On February 20, 1958, the School Board and the Superintendent of Schools filed a petition in the District Court seeking a postponement of their program for desegregation. Their position in essence was that because of extreme public hostility, which they stated had been engendered largely by the official attitudes and actions of the Governor and the Legislature, the maintenance of a sound educational program at Central High School, with the Negro students in attendance would be impossible. The Board therefore proposed that the Negro students already admitted to the school be withdrawn and sent to segregated schools, and that all further steps to carry out the Board's desegregation program be postponed for a period later suggested by the Board to be two and one-half years.

After a hearing the District Court granted the relief requested by the Board. Among other things the court found that the past year at Central High School had been attended by conditions of "chaos, bedlam and turmoil"; that there were "repeated incidents of more or less serious violence directed against the Negro students and their property"; that there was "tension and unrest among the school's administrators, the class-room teachers, the pupils, and the latters' parents, which inevitably had an adverse effect upon the educational program"; that a school official was threatened with violence; that a "serious financial burden" had been cast on the School District; that the education of the students had suffered "and under existing conditions will continue to suffer"; that the Board would continue to need "military assistance or its equivalent"; that the local police department would not be able "to detail enough men to afford the necessary protection"; and that the situation was "intolerable." . . .

The District Court's judgment was dated June 20, 1958. . . . The Court of Appeals . . . after convening in special session on August 4 and hearing the appeal, reversed the District Court. . . .

In affirming the judgment of the Court of Appeals which reversed the District Court we have accepted without reservation the position of the School Board, the Superintendent of Schools, and their counsel that they displayed entire good faith in the conduct of these proceedings and in dealing with the unfortunate and distressing sequence of events which has been outlined. We likewise have accepted the findings of the District Court as to the conditions at Central High School during the 1957–1958 school year, and also the findings that the educational progress of all the students, white and colored, of that school has suffered and will continue to suffer if the conditions which prevailed last year are permitted to continue.

The significance of these findings, however, is to be considered in light of the fact, indisputably revealed by the record before us, that the conditions they depict are directly traceable to the actions of legislators and executive officials of the State of Arkansas, taken in their official capacities, which reflect their own determination to resist this Court's decision in the *Brown* case and which have brought about violent resistance to that decision in Arkansas. In its petition for certiorari filed in this Court, the School Board itself describes the situation in this language: "The legislative, executive, and judicial departments of the state government opposed the desegregation of Little Rock schools by enacting laws, calling out troops, making statements vilifying federal law and federal courts, and failing to utilize state law enforcement agencies and judicial processes to maintain public peace."

One may well sympathize with the position of the Board in the face of the frustrating conditions which have confronted it, but, regardless of the Board's good faith, the actions of the other state agencies responsible for those conditions compel us to reject the Board's legal position. Had Central High School been under the direct management of the State itself, it could hardly be suggested that those immediately in charge of the school should be heard to assert their own good faith as a legal excuse for delay in implementing the constitutional rights of these respondents, when vindication of those rights was rendered difficult or impossible by the actions of other state officials. The situation here is in no different posture because the members of the School Board and the Superintendent of Schools are local officials; from the point of view of the Fourteenth Amendment, they stand in this litigation as the agents of the State.

The constitutional rights of respondents are not to be sacrificed or yielded to the violence and disorder which have followed upon the actions of the Governor and Legislature. As this Court said some 41 years ago in a unanimous opinion in a case involving another aspect of racial segregation: "It is urged that this proposed segregation will promote the public peace by preventing race conflicts. Desirable as this is, and important as is the preservation of the public peace, this aim cannot be accomplished by laws or ordinances which deny rights created or protected by the federal Constitution." *Buchanan* v. *Warley*, 245 US 60. . . . Thus law and order are not here to be preserved by depriving the Negro children of their constitutional rights. The record before us clearly establishes that the growth of the Board's difficulties to a magnitude beyond its unaided power to control is the product of state action. Those difficulties, as counsel for the Board forthrightly conceded on the oral argument in this Court, can also be brought under control by state action.

The controlling legal principles are plain. The command of the Fourteenth Amendment is that no "State" shall deny to any person within its jurisdiction the equal protection of the laws. "A State acts by its legislative, its executive, or its judicial authorities. It can act in no other way. The constitutional provision, therefore, must mean that no agency of the State, or of the officers or agents by whom its powers are exerted, shall deny to any person within its jurisdiction the equal protection of the laws. Whoever, by virtue of public position under a State government . . . denies or takes away the equal protection of the laws, violates the constitutional inhibition; and as he acts in the name and for the State, and is clothed with the State's power, his act is that of the State. This must be so, or the constitutional prohibition has no meaning." *Ex parte Virginia,* 100 US 339. . . . Thus the prohibitions of the Fourteenth Amendment extend to all action of the State denying equal protection of the laws; whatever the agency of the State taking the action. . . . In short, the constitutional rights of children not to be discriminated against in school admission on grounds of race or color declared by this Court in the *Brown* case can neither be nullified openly and directly by state legislators or state executive or judicial officers, nor nullified indirectly by them through evasive schemes for segregation whether attempted "ingeniously or ingenuously." . . .

What has been said, in the light of the facts developed, is enough to dispose of the case. However, we should answer the premise of the actions of the Governor and Legislature that they are not bound by our holding in the *Brown* case. It is necessary only to recall some basic constitutional propositions which are settled doctrine.

Article VI of the Constitution makes the Constitution the "supreme Law of the Land." In 1803, Chief Justice Marshall, speaking for a unanimous Court, referring to the Constitution as "the fundamental and paramount law of the nation," declared in the notable case of *Marbury* v. *Madison,* 1 Cranch 137, that "It is emphatically the province and duty of the judicial department to say what the law is." This decision declared the basic principle that the federal judiciary is supreme in the exposition of the law of the Constitution, and that principle has ever since been respected by this Court and the country as a permanent and indispensable feature of our constitutional system. It follows that the interpretation of the Fourteenth Amendment enunciated by this Court in the *Brown* case is the supreme law of the land, and Art. VI of the Constitution makes it of binding effect on the States, "any Thing in the Constitution or Laws of any State to the Contrary notwithstanding." Every state legislator and executive and judicial officer is solemnly committed by oath taken pursuant to Art. VI, ¶ 3 "to support this Constitution." Chief Justice Taney, speaking for a unanimous Court in 1859, said that this requirement reflected the framers' "anxiety to preserve it [the Constitution] in full force, in all its powers, and to guard against resistance to or evasion of its authority, on the part of a State." *Ableman* v. *Booth,* 21 How. 506. . . .

No state legislator or executive or judicial officer can war against the Constitution without violating his undertaking to support it. Chief Justice Marshall spoke for a unanimous Court in saying that: "If the legislatures of the several states may, at will, annul the judgments of the courts of the United States, and destroy the rights acquired under those judgments, the Constitution itself becomes a solemn mockery. . . ." *United States* v. *Peters,* 5 Cranch 115. A Governor who asserts a power to nullify a federal court order is similarly restrained. If he had such power, said Chief Justice Hughes, in 1932, also for a unanimous Court, "it is manifest that the fiat of a state Governor, and not the Constitution of the United States, would be the supreme law of the land; that the restrictions of the Federal Constitution upon the exercise of state power would be but impotent phrases. . . ." *Sterling* v. *Constantin,* 287 US 378.

It is, of course, quite true that the responsibility for public education is primarily the concern of the States, but it is equally true that such responsibilities, like all other state activity, must be exercised consistently with federal constitutional requirements as they apply to state action. The Constitution created a government dedicated to equal justice under law. The Fourteenth Amendment embodied and emphasized that ideal. State support of segregated schools through any arrangement, management, funds, or property cannot be squared with the Amendment's command that no State shall deny to any person within its jurisdiction the equal protection of the laws. The right of a student not to be segregated on racial grounds in schools so maintained is indeed so fundamental and pervasive that it is embraced in the concept of due process of law. *Bolling* v. *Sharpe,* 347 US 497. The basic decision in *Brown* was unanimously reached by this Court only after the case had been briefed and twice argued and the issues had been given the most serious consideration. Since the first *Brown* opinion three new Justices have come to the Court. They are at one with the Justices still on the Court who participated in that basic decision as to its correctness, and that decision is now unanimously reaffirmed. The principles announced in that decision and the obedience of the States to them, according to the command of the Constitution, are indispensable for the protection of the freedoms guaranteed by our fundamental charter for all of us. Our constitutional ideal of equal justice under law is thus made a living truth.

SEPARATION OF CHURCH AND STATE

The first clause of the Bill of Rights protects against laws "respecting an establishment of religion." The Supreme Court's interpretation of this clause has engendered considerable public controversy because the course of decision has been erratic, the stakes are large (state and federal aid to parochial schools), and religion is an inherently divisive issue. Although the Court sustained Sunday closing or "blue laws," released-time programs, and publicly subsidized bus rides to parochial schools as not violating the First Amendment, it struck down a non-sectarian school prayer that was prescribed by state authorities, thereby touching off demagogic howls that God has been declared unconstitutional, and alarm among usually responsible critics that religious observance had been jeopardized. The Court's decision, however impolitic or inconsistent with early cases, was in keeping with the intentions of the First Amendment's framers to bar any government aid to religion, however impartial or nonpreferential in character. The purpose of the clause against establishments is to protect the government from the ravages of sectarian strife, to promote religious vitality by keeping participation on a voluntary basis and shielding it against government interference, and to safeguard the right to worship as one pleases, if one pleases.

Engle *v.* Vitale

Opinion of the Court by Mr. Justice Black

THE respondent Bcard of Education of Union Free School District No. 9, New Hyde Park, New York, acting in its official capacity under state law, directed the School District's principal to cause the following prayer to be said aloud by each class in the presence of a teacher at the beginning of each school day:

> Almighty God, we acknowledge our dependence upon Thee, and we beg Thy blessings upon us, our parents, our teachers and our country.

This daily procedure was adopted on the recommendation of the State Board of Regents, a governmental agency created by the State Constitution to which the New York Legislature has granted broad supervisory, executive, and legislative powers over the State's public school system. These state officials composed the prayer which they recommended and published as a part of their "Statement on Moral and Spiritual Training in the Schools," saying: "We believe that this Statement will be subscribed to by all men and women of good will, and we call upon all of them to aid in giving life to our program."

Shortly after the practice of reciting the Regents' prayer was adopted by the School District, the parents of ten pupils brought this action in a New York State Court insisting that use of this official prayer in the public schools was contrary to the beliefs, religions, or religious practices of both themselves and their children. Among other things, these parents challenged the constitutionality of both the state law authorizing the School District to direct the use of prayer in public schools and the School District's regulation ordering the recitation of this particular prayer on the ground that these actions of official governmental agencies violate that part of the First Amendment of the Federal Constitution which commands that "Congress shall make no law respecting an establishment of religion"—a command which was "made applicable to the State of New York by the Fourteenth Amendment of the said Constitution." The New York Court of Appeals, over the dissents of Judges Dye and Fuld, sustained an order of the lower state courts which had upheld the power of New York to use the Regents' prayer as a part of the daily procedures of its public schools so long as the schools did not compel any pupil to join in the prayer over his or his parents' objection. We granted certiorari to review this important decision involving rights protected by the First and Fourteenth Amendments.

We think that by using its public school system to encourage recitation of the Regents' prayer, the State of New York has adopted a practice wholly inconsistent with the Establishment Clause. There can, of course, be no doubt that New York's program of daily classroom invocation of God's blessings as prescribed in the Regents' prayer is a religious activity. It is a solemn avowal of divine faith and supplication for the blessings of the Almighty. The nature of such a prayer has always been religious, none of the respondents has denied this and the trial court expressly so found:

The religious nature of prayer was recognized by Jefferson and has been concurred in by theological writers, the United States Supreme Court and state courts and administrative officials, including New York's Commissioner of Education. A committee of the New York Legislature has agreed.

The Board of Regents as *amicus curiae,* the respondents and intervenors all concede the religious nature of prayer, but seek to distinguish this prayer because it is based on our spiritual heritage. * * *

The petitioners contend among other things that the state laws requiring or permitting use of the Regents' prayer must be struck down as a violation of the Establishment Clause because that prayer was composed by governmental officials as a part of a governmental program to further religious beliefs. For this reason, petitioners argue, the State's use of the Regents' prayer in its public school system breaches the constitutional wall of separation between Church and State. We agree with that contention since we think that the constitutional prohibition against laws respecting an establishment of religion must at least mean that in this country it is no part of the business of government to compose official prayers for any group of the American people to recite as a part of a religious program carried on by government.

It is a matter of history that this very practice of establishing governmentally composed prayers for religious services was one of the reasons which caused many of our early colonists to leave England and seek religious freedom in America. The Book of Common Prayer, which was created under governmental direction and which was approved by Acts of Parliament in 1548 and 1549, set out in minute detail the accepted form and content of prayer and other religious ceremonies to be used in the established, tax-supported Church of England. The controversies over the Book and what should be its content repeatedly threatened to disrupt the peace of that country as the accepted forms of prayer in the established church changed with the views of the particular ruler that happened to be in control at the time. Powerful groups representing some of the varying religious views of the people struggled among themselves to impress their particular views upon the Government and obtain amendments of the Book more suitable to their respective notions of how religious services should be conducted in order that the official religious establishment would advance their particular religious beliefs. Other groups, lacking the necessary political power to influence the Government on the matter, decided to leave England and its established church and seek freedom in America from England's governmentally ordained and supported religion.

It is an unfortunate fact of history that when some of the very groups which had most strenuously opposed the established Church of England found themselves sufficiently in control of colonial governments in this country to write their own prayers into law, they passed laws making their own religion the official religion of their respective colonies. Indeed, as late as the time of the Revolutionary War, there were established churches in at least eight of the thirteen former colonies and established religions in at least four of the other five. But the successful Revolution against English political domination was shortly followed by intense opposition to the practice of establishing religion by law. This opposition crystallized rapidly into an effective political force in Virginia where the minority religious groups such as Presbyterians, Lutherans, Quakers and Baptists had gained such strength that the adherents to the established Episcopal Church were actually a minority themselves. In 1785–1786, those opposed to the established Church, led by James Madison and Thomas Jefferson, who, though themselves not members of any of these dissenting religious groups, opposed all religious establishments by law on grounds of principle, obtained the enactment of the famous "Virginia Bill for Religious Liberty" by which all religious groups were placed on an equal footing so far as the State was concerned. Similar though less far-reaching legislation was being considered and passed in other States.

By the time of the adoption of the Constitution, our history shows that there was a widespread awareness among many Americans of the dangers of a union of Church and State. These people knew, some of them from bitter personal experience, that one of the greatest dangers to the freedom of the individual to worship in his own way lay in the Government's placing its official stamp of approval upon one particular kind of prayer or one particular form of religious services. They knew the anguish, hardship and bitter strife that could come when zealous religious groups struggled with one another to obtain the Government's stamp of approval from each King, Queen, or Protector that came to temporary power. The Constitution was intended to avert a part of this danger by leaving the government of this country in the hands of the people rather than in the hands of any monarch. But this safeguard was not enough. Our Founders were no more willing to let the content of their prayers and their privilege of praying whenever they pleased be influenced by the ballot box than they were to let these vital matters of personal conscience depend upon the succession of monarchs. The First Amendment was added to the Constitution to stand as a guarantee that neither the power nor the prestige of the Federal Government would be used to control, support or influence the kinds of prayer the American people can say

—that the people's religions must not be subjected to the pressures of government for change each time a new political administration is elected to office. Under that Amendment's prohibition against governmental establishment of religion, as reinforced by the provisions of the Fourteenth Amendment, government in this country, be it state or federal, is without power to prescribe by law any particular form of prayer which is to be used as an official prayer in carrying on any program of governmentally sponsored religious activity.

There can be no doubt that New York's state prayer program officially establishes the religious beliefs embodied in the Regents' prayer. The respondents' argument to the contrary, which is largely based upon the contention that the Regents' prayer is "nondenominational" and the fact that the program, as modified and approved by state courts, does not require all pupils to recite the prayer but permits those who wish to do so to remain silent or be excused from the room, ignores the essential nature of the program's constitutional defects. Neither the fact that the prayer may be denominationally neutral, nor the fact that its observance on the part of the students is voluntary can serve to free it from the limitations of the Establishment Clause, as it might from the Free Exercise Clause, of the First Amendment, both of which are operative against the States by virtue of the Fourteenth Amendment. Although these two clauses may in certain instances overlap, they forbid two quite different kinds of governmental encroachment upon religious freedom. The Establishment Clause, unlike the Free Exercise Clause, does not depend upon any showing of direct governmental compulsion and is violated by the enactment of laws which establish an official religion whether those laws operate directly to coerce nonobserving individuals or not. This is not to say, of course, that laws officially prescribing a particular form of religious worship do not involve coercion of such individuals. When the power, prestige and financial support of government is placed behind a particular religious belief, the indirect coercive pressure upon religious minorities to conform to the prevailing officially approved religion is plain. But the purposes underlying the Establishment Clause go much further than that. Its first and most immediate purpose rested on the belief that a union of government and religion tends to destroy government and to degrade religion. The history of governmentally established religion, both in England and in this country, showed that whenever government had allied itself with one particular form of religion, the inevitable result had been that it had incurred the hatred, disrespect and even contempt of those who held contrary beliefs. That same history showed that many people had lost their respect for any religion that had relied upon the support of government to spread its faith. The Establishment Clause thus stands as an expression of principle on the part of the Founders of our Constitution that religion is too personal, too sacred, too holy, to permit its "unhallowed perversion" by a civil magistrate. Another purpose of the Establishment Clause rested upon an awareness of the historical fact that governmentally established religions and religious persecutions go hand in hand. The Founders knew that only a few years after the Book of Common Prayer became the only accepted form of religious services in the established Church of England, an Act of Uniformity was passed to compel all Englishmen to attend those services and to make it a criminal offense to conduct or attend religious gatherings of any other kind—a law which was consistently flouted by dissenting religious groups in England and which contributed to widespread persecutions of people like John Bunyan who persisted in holding "unlawful [religious] meetings * * * to the great disturbance and distraction of the good subjects of this kingdom. * * *" And they knew that similar persecutions had received the sanction of law in several of the colonies in this country soon after the establishment of official religions in those colonies. It was in large part to get completely away from this sort of systematic religious persecution that the Founders brought into being our Nation, our Constitution, and our Bill of Rights with its prohibition against any governmental establishment of religion. The New York laws officially prescribing the Regents' prayer are inconsistent with both the purposes of the Establishment Clause and with the Establishment Clause itself.

It has been argued that to apply the Constitution in such a way as to prohibit state laws respecting an establishment of religious services in public schools is to indicate a hostility toward religion or toward prayer. Nothing, of course, could be more wrong. The history of man is inseparable from the history of religion. And perhaps it is not too much to say that since the beginning of that history many people have devoutly believed that "More things are wrought by prayer than this world dreams of." It was doubtless largely due to men who believed this that there grew up a sentiment that caused men to leave the cross-currents of officially established state religions and religious persecution in Europe and come to this country filled with the hope that they could find a place in which they could pray when they pleased to the God of their faith in the language they chose. And there were men of this same faith in the power of prayer who led the fight for adoption of our Constitution and also for our Bill of Rights with the very guarantees of religious freedom that forbid the sort of governmental activity which New York has attempted here. These men knew that the First Amendment, which tried to put an end to governmental control of religion and of prayer, was not written to destroy either. They knew rather that it was written to quiet well-justified fears which nearly all of them felt arising out of an awareness that governments of the past had shackled men's tongues to make them speak only the religious thoughts that government wanted them to speak and to pray only to the God that government wanted them to pray to. It is neither sacrilegious nor anti-religious to say that each separate government in this country should stay out of the business of writing or sanctioning official prayers and leave that purely religious function to the people themselves and to those the people choose to look to for religious guidance.*

It is true that New York's establishment of its Regents' prayer as

---

* There is of course nothing in the decision reached here that is inconsistent with the fact that school children and others are officially encouraged to express love for our country by reciting historical documents such as the Declaration of Independence which contain references to the Deity or by singing officially espoused anthems which include the composer's professions of faith in a Supreme Being, or with the fact that there are many manifestations in our public life of belief in God. Such patriotic or ceremonial occasions bear no true resemblance to the unquestioned religious exercise that the State of New York has sponsored in this instance.

an officially approved religious doctrine of that State does not amount to a total establishment of one particular religious sect to the exclusion of all others—that, indeed, the governmental endorsement of that prayer seems relatively insignificant when compared to the governmental encroachments upon religion which were commonplace 200 years ago. To those who may subscribe to the view that because the Regents' official prayer is so brief and general there can be no danger to religious freedom in its governmental establishment, however, it may be appropriate to say in the words of James Madison, the author of the First Amendment:

[I]t is proper to take alarm at the first experiment on our liberties. * * * Who does not see that the same authority which can establish Christianity, in exclusion of all other Religions, may establish with the same ease any particular sect of Christians, in exclusion of all other Sects? That the same authority which can force a citizen to contribute three pence only of his property for the support of any one establishment, may force him to conform to any other establishment in all cases whatsoever?

The judgment of the Court of Appeals of New York is reversed and the cause remanded for further proceedings not inconsistent with this opinion.

Reversed and remanded.

Mr. Justice FRANKFURTER took no part in the decision of this case.

Mr. Justice WHITE took no part in the consideration or decision of this case.

Mr. Justice DOUGLAS, concurring.

Mr. Justice STEWART's Dissent

A local school board in New York has provided that those pupils who wish to do so may join in a brief prayer at the beginning of each school day, acknowledging their dependence upon God and asking His blessing upon them and upon their parents, their teachers, and their country. The Court today decides that in permitting this brief non-denominational prayer the school board has violated the Constitution of the United States. I think this decision is wrong.

The Court does not hold, nor could it, that New York has interfered with the free exercise of anybody's religion. For the state courts have made clear that those who object to reciting the prayer must be entirely free of any compulsion to do so, including any "embarrassments and pressures." Cf. West Virginia State Board of Education v. Barnette, 319 U.S. 624, 63 S.Ct. 1178, 87 L.Ed. 1628. But the Court says that in permitting school children to say this simple prayer, the New York authorities have established "an official religion."

With all respect, I think the Court has misapplied a great constitutional principle. I cannot see how an "official religion" is established by letting those who want to say a prayer say it. On the contrary, I think that to deny the wish of these school children to join in reciting this prayer is to deny them the opportunity of sharing in the spiritual heritage of our Nation.

The Court's historical review of the quarrels over the Book of Common Prayer in England throws no light for me on the issue before us in this case. England had then and has now an established church. Equally unenlightening, I think, is the history of the early establishment and later rejection of an official church in our own States. For we deal here not with the establishment of a state church, which would, of course, be constitutionally impermissible, but with whether school children who want to begin their day by joining in prayer must be prohibited from doing so. Moreover, I think that the Court's task, in this as in all areas of constitutional adjudication, is not responsibly aided by the uncritical invocation of metaphors like the "wall of separation," a phrase nowhere to be found in the Constitution. What is relevant to the issue here is not the history of an established church in sixteenth century England or in eighteenth century America, but the history of the religious traditions of our people, reflected in countless practices of the institutions and officials of our government.

At the opening of each day's Session of this Court we stand, while one of our officials invokes the protection of God. Since the days of John Marshall our Crier has said, "God save the United States and this Honorable Court." Both the Senate and the House of Representatives open their daily Sessions with prayer. Each of our Presidents, from George Washington to John F. Kennedy, has upon assuming his Office asked the protection and help of God.

The Court today says that the state and federal governments are without constitutional power to prescribe any particular form of words to be recited by any group of the American people on any subject touching religion. The third stanza of "The Star-Spangled Banner," made our National Anthem by Act of Congress in 1931, contains these verses:

> Blest with victory and peace, may the heav'n rescued land
>   Praise the Pow'r that hath made and preserved us a nation!
> Then conquer we must, when our cause it is just,
>   And this be our motto 'In God is our Trust.'

In 1954 Congress added a phrase to the Pledge of Allegiance to the Flag so that it now contains the words "one Nation *under God*, indivisible, with liberty and justice for all." In 1952 Congress enacted legislation calling upon the President each year to proclaim a National Day of Prayer. Since 1865 the words "IN GOD WE TRUST" have been impressed on our coins.

Countless similar examples could be listed, but there is no need to belabor the obvious. It was all summed up by this Court just ten years ago in a single sentence: "We are a religious people whose institutions presuppose a Supreme Being." Zorach v. Clauson, 343 U.S. 306, 313, 72 S.Ct. 679, 684, 96 L.Ed. 954.

I do not believe that this Court, or the Congress, or the President has by the actions and practices I have mentioned established an "official religion" in violation of the Constitution. And I do not believe the State of New York has done so in this case. What each has done has been to recognize and to follow the deeply entrenched and highly cherished spiritual traditions of our Nation—traditions which come down to us from those who almost two hundred years ago avowed their "firm reliance on the Protection of Divine Providence" when they proclaimed the freedom and independence of this brave new world.

I dissent.

FAIR TRIAL AND EQUAL JUSTICE FOR

THE CRIMINALLY ACCUSED

Due process of law lies at the core of the idea of equal justice. The historic purpose of due process is to guarantee fair and regularized procedures by which to determine whether life can be snuffed out or liberty abridged. In a free society, respecting the dignity of all men, the law enforcement process is vigilantly protected against abuse. It is more important that guilt or innocence be fairly judged than that the guilty be punished; a lesser evil, as Justice Holmes remarked, that some criminals should escape than that the government "should play an ignoble role." The fact is that fair and regularized procedures are crucial to the survival of all our most treasured rights. A man's home is not his "castle," his property is not his own, his right to express his convictions or to worship his God is jeopardized, if he can be searched, arrested, and imprisoned unjustly. Because the history of freedom is in large measure the history of procedure, most of the provisions of the Bill of Rights concern procedural matters. The following case illustrates the work of the Supreme Court in enforcing the requirements of due process of law against state violation.

Chambers v. Florida

Opinion of the Court by Mr. Justice Black

THE GRAVE QUESTION presented by the petition for certiorari, granted *in forma pauperis*, is whether proceedings in which confes-

Chambers v. Florida, 309 U. S. 227 (1940).

sions were utilized, and which culminated in sentences of death upon four young negro men in the State of Florida, failed to afford the safeguard of that due process of law guaranteed by the Fourteenth Amendment. . . .

First. The State of Florida challenges our jurisdiction to look behind the judgments below claiming that the issues of fact upon which petitioners base their claim that due process was denied them have been fully determined because passed upon by a jury. However, use by a State of an improperly obtained confession may constitute a denial of due process of law as guaranteed in the Fourteenth Amendment. Since petitioners have reasonably asserted the right under the federal Constitution to have their guilt or innocence of a capital crime determined without reliance upon confessions obtained by means proscribed by the due process clause of the Fourteenth Amendment, we must determine independently whether petitioners' confessions were so obtained, by review of the facts upon which that issue necessarily turns.

Second. The record shows—

About nine o'clock on the night of Saturday, May 13, 1933, Robert Darsey, an elderly white man, was robbed, and murdered in Pompano, Florida, a small town in Broward County about twelve miles from Fort Lauderdale, the County seat. The opinion of the Supreme Court of Florida affirming petitioners' conviction for this crime stated that "It was one of those crimes that induced an enraged community. . . ." And, as the dissenting judge pointed out, "The murder and robbery of the elderly Mr. Darsey . . . was a most dastardly and atrocious crime. It naturally aroused great and well justified public indignation."

Between 9:30 and 10 o'clock after the murder, petitioner Charlie Davis was arrested, and within the next twenty-four hours from twenty-five to forty negroes living in the community, including petitioners Williamson, Chambers, and Woodward, were arrested without warrants and confined in the Broward County jail, at Fort Lauderdale. . . .

It is clear from the evidence of both the State and petitioners that from Sunday, May 14, to Saturday, May 20, the thirty to forty negro suspects were subjected to questioning and cross questioning (with the exception that several of the suspects were in Dade County jail over one night). From the afternoon of Saturday, May 20, until sunrise of the 21st, petitioners and possibly one or two others underwent persistent and repeated questioning. The Supreme Court of Florida said the questioning "was in progress several days and all night before the confessions were secured" and referred to the last night as an "all night vigil." The sheriff who supervised the procedure of continued interrogation testified that he questioned the prisoners "in the day time all the week," but did not question them during any night before the all night vigil of Saturday, May 20, because after having "questioned them all day . . . [he] was tired." Other evidence of the State was "that the officers of Broward County were in that jail almost continually during the whole week questioning these boys, and other boys, in connection with this" case.

The process of repeated questioning took place in the jailer's quarters on the fourth floor of the jail. During the week following their arrest and until their confessions were finally acceptable to the State's Attorney in the early dawn of Sunday, May 21st, petitioners and their fellow prisoners were led one at a time from their cells to the questioning room, quizzed, and returned to their cells to await another turn. So far as appears, the prisoners at no time during the week were permitted to see or confer with counsel or a single friend or relative. When carried singly from his cell and subjected to questioning, each found himself, a single prisoner, surrounded in a fourth floor jail room by four to ten men, the county sheriff, his deputies, a convict guard, and other white officers and citizens of the community.

The testimony is in conflict as to whether all four petitioners were continually threatened and physically mistreated until they finally, in hopeless desperation and fear of their lives, agreed to confess on Sunday morning just after daylight. Be that as it may, it is certain that by Saturday, May 20th, five days of continued questioning had elicited no confession. Admittedly, a concentration of effort—directed against a small number of prisoners including petitioners—on the part of the questioners, principally the sheriff and Williams, the convict guard, began about 3:30 that Saturday afternoon. From that hour on, with only short intervals for food and rest for the questioners—"They all stayed up all night." "They bring one of them at a time backwards and forwards . . . until they confessed." . . .

Sometime in the early hours of Sunday, the 21st, probably about 2:30 A.M., Woodward apparently "broke"—as one of the state's witnesses put it— . . . The State's Attorney was awakened at his home, and called to the jail. He came, but was dissatisfied with the confession of Woodward which he took down in writing at that time, and said something like "tear this paper up, that isn't what I want, when you get something worth while call me." . . .

Just before sunrise, the state officials got something "worthwhile" from petitioners which the State's Attorney would "want"; again he was called; he came; in the presence of those who carried on and witnessed the all-night questioning, he caused his questions and petitioners' answers to be stenographically reported. These are the confessions utilized by the State to obtain the judgments upon which petitioners were sentenced to death. No formal charges had been brought before the confessions. . . . And from arrest until sentenced to death, petitioners were never—either in jail or in court—wholly removed from the constant observation, influence, custody and control of those whose persistent pressure brought about the sunrise confessions. . . .

Third. The scope and operation of the Fourteenth Amendment have been fruitful sources of controversy in our constitutional history. However, in view of its historical setting and wrongs which called it into being, the due process provision of the Fourteenth Amendment —just as that in the Fifth—has led few to doubt that it was intended to guarantee procedural standards adequate and appropriate, then and thereafter, to protect, at all times, people charged with or suspected of crime by those holding positions of power and authority. . . .

The determination to preserve an accused's right to procedural due process sprang in large part from knowledge of the historical truth that the rights and liberties of peoples accused of crime could not be safely entrusted to secret inquisitorial processes. The testimony of centuries, in governments of varying kinds over populations of different races and beliefs, stood as proof that physical and mental torture and coercion had brought about the tragically unjust sacrifices of some who were the noblest and most useful of their generations. The rack, the thumbscrew, the wheel, solitary confinement, protracted questioning and cross questioning, and other ingenious forms of entrapment of the helpless and unpopular had left their wake of mutilated bodies and shattered minds along the way to the cross, the guillotine, the stake and the hangman's noose. And they who have suffered most from secret and dictatorial proceedings have almost always been the poor, the ignorant, the numerically weak, the friendless, and the powerless.

This requirement—of conforming to fundamental standards of procedure in criminal trials—was made operative against the States by the Fourteenth Amendment. . . .

Here, the record develops a sharp conflict upon the issue of physical violence and mistreatment, but shows, without conflict, the dragnet methods of arrest on suspicion without warrant, and the protracted questioning and cross questioning of these ignorant young colored tenant farmers by state officers and other white citizens, in a fourth floor jail room, where as prisoners they were without friends, advisers or counselors, and under circumstances calculated to break the strongest nerves and the stoutest resistance. Just as our decision in *Brown* v. *Mississippi*, 297 U.S. 278, is based upon the fact that the confessions were the result of compulsion, so in the present case, the admitted practices were such as to justify the statement that "The undisputed facts showed that compulsion was applied." . . .

. . . To permit human lives to be forfeited upon confessions thus obtained would make of the constitutional requirement of due process of law a meaningless symbol.

We are not impressed by the argument that law enforcement methods such as those under review are necessary to uphold our laws. The Constitution proscribes such lawless means irrespective of the end. And this argument flouts the basic principle that all people must stand on an equality before the bar of justice in every American court. Today, as in ages past, we are not without tragic proof that the exalted power of some governments to punish manufactured crime dictatorially is the handmaid of tyranny. Under our constitutional system, courts stand against any winds that blow as havens of refuge for those who might otherwise suffer because they are non-conforming victims of prejudice and public excitement. Due process of law, preserved for all by our Constitution, commands that no such practice as that disclosed by this record shall send any accused to his death. No higher duty, no more solemn responsibility, rests upon this Court, than that of translating into living law and maintaining this constitutional shield deliberately planned and inscribed for the benefit of every human being subject to our Constitution—of whatever race, creed, or persuasion.

The Supreme Court of Florida was in error and its judgment is
Reversed.

THE BILL OF RIGHTS AND THE

COMMUNIST PROBLEM

During the Cold War, claims of national security subordinated those of personal liberty—although the purpose of security is to safeguard liberty, the Supreme Court inclined to the view that the Bill of Rights should not straitjacket the government's struggle with Communist subversion. The Court in the 1957 Yates case—after there had been 145 indictments and 89 convictions—belatedly construed the Smith Act to preclude prosecution of party leaders who advocate an abstract doctrine of forcible overthrow of the government in contrast to advocacy of action for forcible overthrow. This ruling halted prosecutions under the provisions against conspiracy to organize, teach, and advocate forcible overthrow. But in 1961 the Court, by a five to four vote, sustained the conviction of Junius Scales, a party organizer, under the "membership clause" of the Smith Act; on the same day, however, the Court quixotically reversed the conviction of John F. Noto in an opinion that has made it practically impossible for the government to secure any further convictions under that clause. Scales, who defected from the party after Hungary, is now serving a six-year prison term, the most severe sentence imposed in any Smith Act prosecution. The fact that he had not been charged with any overt acts to overthrow the government (as, indeed, had no defendant in a Smith Act prosecution) explains in part why the dissenting opinion is so bitter. President Robert F. Goheen of Princeton and Reinhold Niebuhr, the Protestant theologian, head a distinguished committee of Americans who seek a Presidential pardon for Scales.

Scales *v.* United States

Opinion of the Court by Mr. Justice Harlan

OUR WRIT issued in this case (358 U.S. 917) to review a judgment of the Court of Appeals (260 F. 2d 21) affirming petitioner's conviction under the so-called membership clause of the Smith Act. 18 U. S. C. § 2385. The Act, among other things, makes a felony the acquisition or holding of knowing membership in any organization which advocates the overthrow of the Government of the United States by force or violence. The indictment charged that from January 1946 to the date of its filing (November 18, 1954) the Communist Party of the United States was such an organization, and that petitioner throughout that period was a member thereof, with knowledge of the Party's illegal purpose and a specific intent to accomplish overthrow "as speedily as circumstances would permit." . . .

CONSTITUTIONAL CHALLENGE TO THE MEMBERSHIP CLAUSE ON ITS FACE

. . . It will bring the constitutional issues into clearer focus to notice first the premises on which the case was submitted to the jury. The jury was instructed that in order to convict it must find that within the three-year limitations period (1) the Communist Party advocated the violent overthrow of the Government, in the sense of present "advocacy of action" to accomplish that end as soon as circumstances were propitious; and (2) petitioner was an "active" member of the Party, and not merely "a nominal, passive, inactive or purely technical" member, with knowledge of the Party's illegal advocacy and a specific intent to bring about violent overthrow "as speedily as circumstances would permit."

The constitutional attack upon the membership clause, as thus construed, is that the statute offends (1) the Fifth Amendment, in that it impermissibly imputes guilt to an individual merely on the basis of his associations and sympathies, rather than because of some concrete personal involvement in criminal conduct; and (2) the First Amendment, in that it infringes on free political expression and association. Subsidiarily, it is argued that the statute cannot be interpreted as including a requirement of a specific intent to accomplish violent overthrow, or as requiring that membership in a proscribed organization must be "active" membership, in the absence of both or either of which it is said the statute becomes *a fortiori* unconstitutional. It is further contended that even if the adjective "active" may properly be implied as a qualification upon the term "member," petitioner's conviction would nonetheless be unconstitutional, because so construed the statute would be impermissibly vague under the Fifth and Sixth Amendments, and so applied would in any event infringe the Sixth Amendment, in that the indictment charged only that Scales was a "member," not an "active" member, of the Communist Party.

STATUTORY CONSTRUCTION

Before reaching petitioner's constitutional claims, we should first ascertain whether the membership clause permissibly bears the construction put upon it below. We think it does.

The trial court's definition of the kind of organizational advocacy that is proscribed was fully in accord with what was held in *Yates* v. *United States*, 354 U.S. 298. And the statute itself requires that a defendant must have knowledge of the organization's illegal advocacy.

The only two elements of the crime, as defined below, about which there is controversy are therefore "specific intent" and "active" membership. As to the former, this Court held in *Dennis* v. *United States*, 341 U.S. 494, 499-500, that even though the "advocacy" and "organizing" provisions of the Smith Act, unlike the "literature" section, did not expressly contain such a specific intent element, such a requirement was fairly to be implied. We think that the reasoning of *Dennis* applies equally to the membership clause, and are left unpersuaded by the distinctions petitioner seeks to draw between this clause and the advocacy and organizing provisions of the Smith Act.

We find hardly greater difficulty in interpreting the membership clause to reach only "active" members. We decline to attribute to Congress a purpose to punish nominal membership, even though accompanied by "knowledge" and "intent," not merely because of the close constitutional questions that such a purpose would raise . . ., but also for two other reasons: It is not to be lightly inferred that Congress intended to visit upon mere passive members the heavy penalties imposed by the Smith Act. Nor can we assume that it was Congress' purpose to allow the quality of the punishable membership to be measured solely by the varying standards of that relationship as subjectively viewed by different organizations. It is more reasonable to believe that Congress contemplated an objective standard fixed by the law itself, thereby assuring an even-handed application of the statute. . . .

We hold that the statute was correctly interpreted by the two lower courts, and now turn to petitioner's basic constitutional challenge.

FIFTH AMENDMENT

In our jurisprudence guilt is personal, and when the imposition of punishment on a status or on conduct can only be justified by reference to the relationship of that status or conduct to other concededly criminal activity (here advocacy of violent overthrow), that relationship must be sufficiently substantial to satisfy the concept of personal guilt in order to withstand attack under the Due Process Clause of the Fifth Amendment. Membership, without more, in an organization engaged in illegal advocacy, it is now said, has not heretofore been recognized by this Court to be such a relationship. This claim stands, and we shall examine it, independently of the claim made under the First Amendment.

Any thought that due process puts beyond the reach of the criminal law all individual associational relationships, unless accompanied by the commission of specific acts of criminality, is dispelled by familiar concepts of the law of conspiracy and complicity. While both are commonplace in the landscape of the criminal law, they are not natural features. Rather they are particular legal concepts manifesting the more general principle that society, having the power to punish dangerous behavior, cannot be powerless against those who work to bring about that behavior. The fact that Congress has not resorted to either of these familiar concepts means only that the enquiry here must direct itself to an analysis of the relationship between the fact of membership and the underlying substantive illegal conduct, in order to determine whether that relationship is indeed too tenuous to permit its use as the basis of criminal liability. In this instance it is an organization which engages in criminal activity, and we can perceive no reason why one who actively and knowingly works in the ranks of that organization, intending to contribute to the success of those specifically illegal activities, should be any more immune from prosecution than he to whom the organization has assigned the task of carrying out the substantive criminal act. Nor should the fact that Congress has focussed here on "membership," the characteristic relationship between an individual and the type of conspiratorial quasi-political associations with the criminal aspect of whose activities Congress was concerned, of itself require the conclusion that the legislature has traveled outside the familiar and permissible bounds of criminal imputability. In truth, the specificity of the proscribed relationship is not necessarily a vice; it provides instruction and warning.

What must be met, then, is the argument that membership, even when accompanied by the elements of knowledge and specific intent, affords an insufficient quantum of participation in the organization's alleged criminal activity, that is, an insufficiently significant form of aid and encouragement to permit the imposition of criminal sanctions on that basis. It must indeed be recognized that a person who merely becomes a member of an illegal organization, by that "act" alone need be doing nothing more than signifying his assent to its purposes and activities on one hand, and providing, on the other, only the sort of moral encouragement which comes from the knowledge that others believe in what the organization is doing. It may indeed be argued that such assent and encouragement do fall short of the concrete, practical impetus given to a criminal enterprise which is lent for instance by a commitment on the part of a conspirator to act in furtherance of that enterprise. A member, as distinguished from a conspirator, may indicate his approval of a criminal enterprise by the very fact of his membership without thereby necessarily committing himself to further it by any act or course of conduct whatever.

In an area of the criminal law which this Court has indicated more than once demands its watchful scrutiny . . . these factors have weight and must be found to be overborne in a total constitutional assessment of the statute. We think, however, they are duly met when the statute is found to reach only "active" members having also a guilty knowledge and intent, and which therefore prevents a conviction on what otherwise might be regarded as merely an expression of sympathy with the alleged criminal enterprise, unaccompanied by any significant action in its support or any commitment to undertake such action.

Thus, given the construction of the membership clause already discussed, we think the factors called for in rendering members criminally responsible for the illegal advocacy of the organization fall within established, and therefore presumably constitutional, standards of criminal imputability.

FIRST AMENDMENT

Little remains to be said concerning the claim that the statute infringes First Amendment freedoms. It was settled in *Dennis* that the advocacy with which we are here concerned is not constitutionally protected speech, and it was further established that a combination to promote such advocacy, albeit under the aegis of what purports to be a political party, is not such association as is protected by the First Amendment. We can discern no reason why membership, when it constitutes a purposeful form of complicity in a group engaging in this same forbidden advocacy, should receive any greater degree of protection from the guarantees of that Amendment.

If it is said that the mere existence of such an enactment tends to inhibit the exercise of constitutionally protected rights, in that it engenders an unhealthy fear that one may find himself unwittingly embroiled in criminal liability, the answer surely is that the statute provides that a defendant must be proven to have knowledge of the proscribed advocacy before he may be convicted. It is, of course, true that quasi-political parties or other groups that may embrace both legal and illegal aims differ from a technical conspiracy, which is defined by its criminal purpose, so that *all* knowing association with the conspiracy is a proper subject for criminal proscription as far as First Amendment liberties are concerned. If there were a similar blanket prohibition of association with a group having both legal and illegal aims, there would indeed be a real danger that legitimate political expression or association would be impaired, but the membership clause, as here construed, does not cut deeper into the freedom of association than is necessary to deal with "the substantive evils that Congress has a right to prevent." *Schenck* v. *United States*, 249 U.S. 47, 52. The clause does not make criminal all association with an organization which has been shown to engage in illegal advocacy. There must be clear proof that a defendant "specifically intend[s] to accomplish [the aims of the organization] by resort to violence." *Noto* v. *United States, post,* at p. 299. Thus the member for whom the organization is a vehicle for the advancement of legitimate aims and policies does not fall within the ban of the statute: he lacks the requisite specific intent "to bring about the overthrow of the government as speedily as circumstances would permit." Such a person may be foolish, deluded, or perhaps merely optimistic, but he is not by this statute made a criminal.

We conclude that petitioner's constitutional challenge must be overruled.

Mr. Justice DOUGLAS'S Dissent

When we allow petitioner to be sentenced to prison for six years for being a "member" of the Communist Party, we make a sharp break with traditional concepts of First Amendment rights and make serious Mark Twain's light-hearted comment that "It is by the goodness of God that in our country we have those three unspeakably precious things: freedom of speech, freedom of conscience, and the prudence never to practice either of them."

Even the Alien and Sedition Laws—shameful reminders of an early chapter in intolerance—never went so far as we go today. They were aimed at conspiracy and advocacy of insurrection and at the publication of "false, scandalous and malicious" writing against the Government, 1 Stat. 596. The Government then sought control over the press "in order to strike at one of the chief sources of disaffection and sedition." Miller, Crisis in Freedom (1951), p. 56. There is here no charge of conspiracy, no charge of any overt act to overthrow the Government by force and violence, no charge of any other criminal act. The charge is being a "member" of the Communist Party, "well-knowing" that it advocated the overthrow of the Government by force and violence, "said defendant intending to bring about such overthrow by force and violence as speedily as circumstances would permit." That falls far short of a charge of conspiracy. Conspiracy rests not in intention alone but in an agreement with one or more others to promote an unlawful project. . . . No charge of any kind or sort of agreement hitherto embraced in the concept of a conspiracy is made here.

We legalize today guilt by association, sending a man to prison when he committed no unlawful act. Today's break with tradition is a serious one. It borrows from the totalitarian philosophy. As stated by O'Brian, National Security and Individual Freedom (1955), pp. 27-28:

The Smith Act of 1940 *made it unlawful* for any person to be or to become a member of or affiliate with any society, group, or assembly which teaches, advocates, or encourages the overthrow or destruction of any government in the United States by force or violence. These statutes [the Smith Act together with a 1920 amendment to the Immigration Law, Act of June 5, 1920, 41 Stat. 1008], therefore, imported into our law the alien doctrine of guilt by association, which up to this time had been regarded as abhorrent and which had never been recognized either by the courts or by the Department of Justice, even during the perils and excitements of the First World War.

The case is not saved by showing that petitioner was an active member. None of the activity constitutes a crime. The record contains evidence that Scales was the Chairman of the North and South Carolina Districts of the Communist Party. He recruited new members into the Party, and promoted the advanced education of selected young Party members in the theory of communism to be undertaken at secret schools. He was a director of one such school. He explained the principles of the Party to an FBI agent who posed as someone interested in joining the Party, and furnished him literature, including articles which criticized in vivid language the American "aggression" in Korea and described American "atrocities" committed on Korean citizens. He once remarked that the Party was setting up underground means of communication, and in 1951 he himself "went underground." At the school of which Scales was director, students were told (by someone else) that one of the Party's weaknesses was in failing to place people in key industrial positions. One witness told of a meeting arranged by Scales at which the staff of the school urged him to remain in his position in an industrial plant rather than return to college. In Scales' presence, students at the school were once shown how to kill a person with a pencil, a device which, it was said, might come in handy on a picket line. Other evidence showed Scales to have made several statements or distributed literature containing implicating passages. Among them were comments to the effect that the Party line was that the Negroes in the South and the working classes should be used to foment a violent revolution; that a Communist government could not be voted into power in this country because the Government controlled communication media, newspapers, the military, and the educational systems, and that force was the only way to achieve the revolution; that if a depression were to come the Communist America would be closer at hand than predicted by William Z. Foster; that the revolution would come within a generation; that it would be easier in the United States than in Russia to effectuate the revolution because of assistance and advice from

Russian Communists. Petitioner at different times said or distributed literature which said that the goals of communism could only be achieved by violent revolution that would have to start internally with the working classes.

Not one single illegal act is charged to petitioner. That is why the essence of the crime covered by the indictment is merely belief—belief in the proletarian revolution, belief in Communist creed. . . . The crime of belief—presently prosecuted—is a carryback to the old law of treason where men were punished for compassing the death of the King. That law, which had been employed for "suppression of political opposition or the expression of ideas or beliefs distasteful to those in power." Hurst, Historic Background of the Treason Clause, 6 Fed. B. J. 305, 307, was rejected here, and the treason clause of our Constitution was "most praised for the reason that it prevented the use of treason trials as an instrument of political faction." *Id.*, 307. Sedition or treason in the realm of politics and heresy in the ecclesiastical field had long centered on *beliefs* as the abhorrent criminal act. The struggle on this side of the Atlantic was to get rid of that concept and to punish men not for what they thought but for overt acts against the peace of the Nation. . . . Our long and painful experience with the law of treason, wholly apart from the First Amendment, should be enough warning that we as a free people should not venture again into the field of prosecuting beliefs.

That was the philosophy behind *Board of Education* v. *Barnette*, 319 U.S. 624, 641-642:

We can have intellectual individualism and the rich cultural diversities that we owe to exceptional minds only at the price of occasional eccentricity and abnormal attitudes. When they are so harmless to others or to the State as those we deal with here, the price is not too great. But freedom to differ is not limited to things that do not matter much. That would be a mere shadow of freedom. The test of its substance is the right to differ as to things that touch the heart of the existing order.

If there is any fixed star in our constitutional constellation, it is that no official, high or petty, can prescribe what shall be orthodox in politics, nationalism, religion, or other matters of opinion or force citizens to confess by word or act their faith therein. If there are any circumstances which permit an exception, they do not now occur to us.

Nothing but beliefs is on trial in this case. They are unpopular and to most of us revolting. But they are nonetheless ideas or dogmas or faiths within the broad framework of the First Amendment. . . . The creed truer to our faith was stated by the Bar Committee headed by Charles E. Hughes which in 1920 protested the refusal of the New York Assembly to seat five members of the Socialist Party:

. . . it is of the essence of the institutions of liberty that it be recognized that guilt is personal and cannot be attributed to the holding of opinion or to mere intent in the absence of overt acts. . . .

Belief in the principle of revolution is deep in our traditions. The Declaration of Independence proclaims it:

whenever any Form of Government becomes destructive of these Ends, it is the Right of the People to alter or to abolish it, and to institute new Government, laying its Foundation on such Principles, and organizing its Powers in such Form, as to them shall seem most likely to effect their Safety and Happiness.

This right of revolution has been and is a part of the fabric of our institutions. . . .

Of course, government can move against those who take up arms against it. Of course, the constituted authority has the right of self-preservation. But we deal in this prosecution of Scales only with the legality of ideas and beliefs, not with overt acts. The Court speaks of the prevention of "dangerous behavior" by punishing those "who work to bring about that behavior." That formula returns man to the dark days when government determined what behavior was "dangerous" and then policed the dissidents for tell-tale signs of advocacy. . . .

In recent years we have been departing, I think, from the theory of government expressed in the First Amendment. We have too often been "balancing" the right of speech and association against other values in society to see if we, the judges, feel that a particular need is more important than those guaranteed by the Bill of Rights. . . .

The trend of history, as Jefferson noted, has been against the rights of man. He wrote that "The natural progress of things is for liberty to yield and government to gain ground." The formula he prepared for a society where ideas flourished was not punishment of the unorthodox but education and enlightenment of the masses. . . . This is the only philosophy consistent with the First Amendment. When belief in an idea is punished as it is today, we sacrifice those ideals and substitute an alien, totalitarian philosophy in their stead. . . .

What we lose by majority vote today may be reclaimed at a future time when the fear of advocacy, dissent, and nonconformity no longer cast a shadow over us.